MW00975230

To Live In His SIGHT

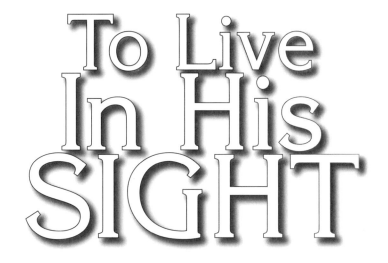

To Live In His SIGHT

A Gospel Guide
to Revival and Reformation

By Leslie Kay

Roseville, CA

Copyright © 2004 by Leslie Kay

Printed in United States of America
All Rights Reserved

Published by Amazing Facts, Inc.
P. O. Box 1058
Roseville, CA 95678-8058
800-538-7275

Other books by Leslie Kay:
Scraps of Wisdom From Grasshopper Junction
Simple Gifts

Co-authored with Jennifer Jill Schwirzer:
A Deep But Dazzling Darkness

Text Editing by Anthony Lester
Cover Design by Steve Miljatovic – Branch 7 Design
Text Design and Layout by Greg Solie – Altamont Graphics

Typeset: 13/15 Minion

Library of Congress Cataloging-in-Publication Data

Kay, Leslie (Leslie Eileen), 1957-
  To live in His sight : a gospel guide to revival and reformation / by Leslie Kay.
    p. cm.
  ISBN 1-58019-181-9 (alk. paper)
  1. Church renewal--Seventh-Day Adventists. 2. Religious awakening--Seventh-Day Adventists. 3. Seventh-Day Adventists--Doctrines. I. Title.

BX6154.K39 2004
243--dc22

                                2004022398

04 05 06 07 08 • 5 4 3 2 1

To Live In His Sight
A Gospel Guide to Revival and Reformation

— FOREWORD —

D o you long for a revival in your relationship with God? Does it seem to you that there could and should be more to your Christian experience than there is right now? Would you like to experience one victory after another in your walk with the Lord? If you answered yes to any of these questions, then this book is for you.

Virtually everyone needs revival. Can we make it happen? No! But we can seek after it. When we hunger and thirst for a relationship with our Lord as we seek for food and water, God promises that we will be filled. He will put us on the pathway to spiritual satisfaction.

Of course, the ultimate pathway to revival leads straight to and through Jesus, who said, "I am the Way." He didn't say that He would show us the way, but that He is "the Way." He is the path, and He is the lamp that illuminates that path. When you truly find Jesus, you will find rock-solid revival in your heart, your spirit, and your entire life. Thankfully, God has also promised that when we seek after Jesus with all of our heart, we will surely find Him (Jeremiah 29:13).

Toward this end, author Leslie Kay has written a powerful yet practical guide that will lead you into a closer walk with Jesus. Within these pages, you're going to find biblical, life-changing help that will open your heart to the indwelling power of the Holy Spirit, that you might be prepared for the soon-coming latter rain.

I invite you to prayerfully read through each eye-opening, beautifully-written chapter and, step-by-step, experience a brand-new, revived relationship with the Way.

Doug Batchelor

President/Speaker
Amazing Facts

THE CALL TO REVIVAL

Chapter One
Revival Essentials

> *"A revival of true godliness among us is the greatest and most urgent of all our needs. To seek this should be our first work."*
> —Ellen G. White, *Selected Messages, Book One* [1]

E zra had a serious problem on his hands. Having recently trudged across 1,600 miles of burning desert from Persia to Jerusalem, to spiritually revive and reorganize Judah following their return from exile, the old priest and scribe was confronted by a contingency of concerned leaders. It was bad enough, they complained, that the people of Israel had been intermarrying with the surrounding pagan tribes, exposing their families and community to faith-destroying "detestable practices" [2] (Ezra 9:1). [3] But the worst of it was that the ones who should have been foremost in setting an example of fidelity— "the priests and the Levites" and "the leaders and officials"— had flagrantly "led the way in this unfaithfulness" (vs. 1, 2).

"Appalled" at his people's persistent spiritual perversity and ingratitude toward God, the old priest tore his clothes and pulled out his hair in a display of abject grief (v. 3). Having attracted a core group of sympathizers, he sat grieving with them until the time of the evening sacrifice, when he fell on his knees, spread his hands in supplication before the Lord, and prayed one of the most heart-rending prayers in the Bible. Though personally

innocent of Israel's grievous sin, he took the part of his erring
people and interceded in their behalf:

> "O my God, I am too ashamed and disgraced
> to lift up my face to you, my God, because our
> sins are higher than our heads and our guilt has
> reached to the heavens. From the days of our
> forefathers until now, our guilt has been great.
> Because of our sins, we and our kings and our
> priests have been subjected to the sword and
> captivity, to pillage and humiliation at the hand
> of foreign kings, as it is today" (Ezra 9:6, 7).

Far from being a superficial repentance inspired by self-
righteous repugnance or a craven fear of punishment, Ezra
sorrowed that his people so faintly appreciated God's mercy
and so little valued the privilege of their high calling:

> "The Lord our God has been gracious in leaving
> us a remnant and giving us a firm place in his
> sanctuary ... Though we are slaves, our God has
> not deserted us in our bondage. He has shown us
> kindness in the sight of the kings of Persia: He
> has granted us new life to rebuild the house of
> our God and repair its ruins, and he has given
> us a wall of protection in Judah and Jerusalem"
> (vs. 8, 9).

Refusing to palliate their guilt, Ezra painted it in its darkest hue
against the brilliant backdrop of God's undeserved goodness. An
astute student of the Bible and his people's history, he reasoned
from cause to effect, putting his finger on the plague spot of
persistent "disregard" of God's express "commands" (vs. 10, 11)—
how could God bless and revive a people who, by their rebellious
attitude and actions, persistently drove Him away?

Touched by his anguish in their behalf and by the pain of their own awakening consciences, "a large crowd of Israelites—men, women, and children—gathered around him. They too wept bitterly" (Ezra 10:1). "In a limited degree they began to realize the heinousness of sin and the horror with which God regards it. They saw the sacredness of the law spoken at Sinai, and many trembled at the thought of their transgressions."[4] Now conscious that they were destitute of inner righteousness, with their denial and defenses stripped away, they frankly confessed, "We have been unfaithful to our God." Laying hold of His righteousness and promise for deliverance, they asserted, "But in spite of this, there is still hope for Israel" (v. 2).

Caught in the unbearable tension created by a dual awareness of God's goodness and their own sinfulness, Israel died to self and was birthed into new life. Revival had come, and it prepared the way for "a wonderful reformation"[5] in which was seen "fruit in keeping with repentance" (Matthew 3:8): a deepening appreciation for God's holy, benevolent character, with a corresponding separation from sin—all within the compassionate context of "a careful consideration for the rights and welfare of every individual concerned."[6]

It's a classic story of corporate revival and reformation that reverberates throughout the biblical record. As we examine it closely, we can identify these essential components:

- It was started by a small core group of spiritually sensitive, mature believers who were as "firm as a rock where right principles [were] involved," yet manifest "compassion and tenderness ... toward those who had sinned, either willfully or through ignorance."[7]
- Having wrestled extensively with their own sinful propensities, this group was able to identify with their erring brothers and sisters, and, in one accord, prayed

and labored as earnestly for their salvation as they did for their own.

- Catalyzed by this Christ-like intercession on their behalf, and the Holy Spirit's application of it to their own hearts, those who were willing were drawn from the periphery of revival into its vibrant center.

- As they examined their lives in the searching light of the Word of God, they became personally convicted of the heinousness of their sin and the sorrow it caused their Lord; as they thoroughly repented and confessed, faith reached out to claim the righteousness of God and His deliverance.

- Reformation followed, as the people internalized the life-changing principles of God's Word, and adjusted their behavior accordingly.

It would be wise to pause, at this point, and fix in our minds a crucial distinction between revival and reformation, to keep us from doing what we are so prone to do—putting the reformation "cart" before the revival "horse." As Ellen White has helpfully explained:

> "Revival and reformation are two different things. Revival signifies *a renewal of spiritual life, a quickening of the powers of mind and heart, a resurrection from spiritual death.* Reformation signifies *a reorganization, a change in ideas and theories, habits and practices.* Reformation will not bring forth the good fruit of righteousness unless it is connected with the revival of the Spirit. Revival and reformation are to do their appointed work, and in doing this work they must blend. [8]

Only the Holy Spirit can orchestrate this necessary blending of renewal and reorganization, and ensure that each does its "appointed work." While we need to recognize that the big picture consistently contains the essential components outlined above, (we'll expand on these components in the following chapters), we can never reduce this to a formula or a program that we "work" at our discretion. Our very important part is to cooperate with the Holy Spirit and assist *Him* in His work of inspiring and establishing "true godliness," or we'll end up with a well-intentioned but inferior human imitation.

And because godliness is literally God-*like*-ness, we need a clear understanding of the character of the One we wish to become like. For this reason, true revival will always be precipitated by a confrontation with the goodness and holiness of God, as we'll see in the following chapter.

Endnotes

1. Ellen G. White, *Selected Messages, Book One*, p. 121.

2. Practices that included such truly "detestable" features as orgiastic fertility rites, self-mutilation, and human sacrifice.

3. All Scripture quotations in this chapter are taken from the New International Version.

4. Ellen G. White, *Prophets and Kings*, p. 622.

5. *Ibid.*

6. *Ibid.*

7. *Ibid.*, p. 623.

8. Ellen G. White, *Selected Messages, Book One*, p. 128 (italics added).

Chapter Two
Where Every Mouth is Silenced

*"It is only as the law of God is restored to its rightful
position that there can be a revival of primitive faith
and godliness among His professed people."*
                    —Ellen G. White, *The Great Controversy*[1]

M ount Sinai looked forbidding enough under
normal circumstances—a tortured spine of earth
thrust against an electric azure sky. But today it
was positively terrifying, as it quaked and reeled at its divine
visitation. Wreathed in an impenetrable cloud, out of which
lightning snaked and thunder reverberated, its base was encased
by a barrier that could be trespassed only on pain of death. As a
deafening, otherworldly trumpet blast summoned the Israelites
to worship, they crept trembling from their tents, only to be
further terrified by the sight of the Lord descending upon the
besieged mountain in flaming fire, which set it smoking like a
furnace. When they felt they could bear the awful grandeur of
the scene no longer, the trumpet rang louder and still louder,
until it suddenly gave way to a silence that was more awful
still. Out of this dreadful silence, the voice of God spoke 10
timeless moral imperatives that, taken together, comprised a
comprehensive "revelation" to humanity "of the will and the
character of its Author."[2]

We who have become accustomed (from a safe distance) to similarly spectacular displays of "shock and awe" might well ask, *What was the point of all the drama? Was God just trying to terrify these poor ex-slaves into submission?* Actually, He was trying to instill within them, and us, a crucial sense of perspective by tearing away the veil and giving us all a glimpse of *reality*. The truth behind our divinely subsidized existence is that God is "holy and just and good" and we are, of ourselves, morally "worthless"—a fact that becomes painfully clear when we stand before the searching gaze of "the Judge of all the earth" (Romans 7:12; 3:12, NIV; Genesis 18:25). Before Sinai's sin-consuming fire, "every mouth" is "silenced," and "the whole world" stands "accountable to God" (Romans 3:19, NIV).

If revival is to take deep root in our lives, and result in thorough reformation, it is imperative that we become conscious of our innate moral bankruptcy. As Ellen White has so logically outlined it, "*The first step in reconciliation to God is the conviction of sin.* 'Sin is the transgression of the law.' 'By the law is the knowledge of sin.' (1 John 3:4; Romans 3:20). In order to see his guilt, the sinner must test his character by God's great standard of righteousness. It is a mirror which shows the perfection of a righteous character and enables him to discern the defects in his own."[3]

This "great standard of righteousness" (which includes every biblical imperative, by extension) is able to function in this capacity because, far from being arbitrary, it derives from the living and authoritative character of God Himself. As Christian ethicist Norman Geisler has noted:

> "The ethical imperatives that God gives are in accord with his unchangeable moral character. That is, God wills what is right in accordance with his own moral attributes. 'Be holy, because I am holy,' the Lord commanded Israel (Lev. 11:45).

'Be perfect, therefore, as your heavenly Father is
perfect,' Jesus said to his disciples (Matt. 5:48). 'It
is impossible for God to lie' (Hebrews 6:18). So we
should not lie either. 'God is love' (1 John 4:16),
and so Jesus said, 'Love your neighbor as yourself'
(Matt. 22:39)."[4]

Before the Fall, the selfless, principled love from which this
standard derives had been innate to humanity, as our hearts
and minds moved in moral synchronism with God's. But with
the entrance of sin, we expelled God's indwelling character, in
which are bound up the very principles of life, and that which
had been intrinsic to humanity became extrinsic. The great
Moral Law of Love and Life that was once *descriptive* of our
inmost beings became *prescriptive*—it no longer spoke of who
we *were*, but of who we *ought to be*. Humanity has ever since
found itself perched on the points of a dilemma consisting of
these two prongs:

"First, that human beings, all over the earth,
have this curious idea that they *ought* to behave
in a certain way, and cannot really get rid of it.
Secondly, that they *do not* in fact behave in that
way. They know the [moral] Law of Nature; they
break it. These two facts are the foundation of all
clear thinking about ourselves and the universe
we live in."[5]

This, then, is our starting place for revival—God is good; we
are not. It's a painful, but necessary wake-up call. Thank God,
He loves us too much to rock us even more deeply into our sin-
drugged stupor. At Sinai, He plants our feet on the very brink
of the yawning chasm that stretches between His transcendent
holiness and our base corruption, that we may lose all hope of
ever bridging it of our own accord.

As we see our "lost condition as violators of God's law," we begin to "realize our need of the atoning blood of Christ," the only avenue through which we can experience "a radical change of heart" and "reformation of life." [6] The tortured ramparts of Sinai give way to the saving contours of Calvary, where Christ bridged the chasm and reconciled us to our righteous Creator.

Endnotes

1. Ellen G. White, *The Great Controversy*, p. 478.

2. *Ibid.* p. 467.

3. *Ibid.* (italics added).

4. Norman Geisler, *Christian Ethics* (Grand Rapids, MI: Baker Book House, 1989), p. 22.

5. C.S. Lewis, *Mere Christianity* (New York: HarperCollins Publishers, 2001), p. 8 (italics added).

6. *The Great Controversy*, p. 468.

Chapter Three
That We May Live in His Sight

> *"Come, and let us return to the Lord; for He has torn, but He will heal us; He has stricken, but He will bind us up. After two days He will revive us; on the third day He will raise us up, that we may live in His sight."*
>
> —Hosea 6:1, 2

The word "revive" is combined from two Latin roots that together mean to *live again*. Webster's expands on this simple definition by further explaining that it means to bring back to life or consciousness; to bring back to a healthy, vigorous, or flourishing condition after a decline.

Decline, both physical and moral, is the perpetual condition of our fallen world; it's the natural default setting of sinful beings who are "all day long, and all the days of our life ... sliding, slipping, falling away—as if God were, to our present consciousness, a smooth inclined plane on which there is no resting." [1] As we discussed in our last chapter, when our primeval parents kicked God out of their consciousness, they left us a legacy of spiritual disorientation and weakness that has rendered us, of ourselves, incapable of knowing and doing God's good and perfect will. Consequently, we are "programmed" to drift away from that which would bring us spiritual and physical life, into that which brings decline and, ultimately, death. (See Romans 3:10–18.)

18

Fortunately, God loves us too much to let us languish in this otherwise hopeless cycle of decline and death. As the verse above explains, He is constantly at work to *revive* us, to make us *live again*—to transform us into spiritually healthy, vigorous, and flourishing reflections of Himself. Though at Sinai, He must cause us to be "torn" and "stricken" to bring us to an awareness of our desperate need, He does so that He may bind up our wounds and heal us, that we may be fitted to "live in His sight."

This He accomplishes at Calvary. Isaiah chapter 53 picks up on the language of our verse to paint a heart-melting portrait of Christ as the Suffering Servant who was "wounded for our transgressions" and "bruised for our iniquities;" for our sakes He was "stricken, smitten by God, and afflicted," that "by His stripes" we may be "healed" (Isaiah 53:5, 4). We are able to be healed, or *revived*, because of what Christ has done for us. As Ellen White has so eloquently expressed it:

> "Christ was treated as we deserve, that we might be treated as He deserves. He was condemned for our sins, in which He had no share, that we might be justified by His righteousness, in which we had no share. He suffered the death which was ours, that we might receive the life which was His. 'With His stripes we are healed.'" [2]

This is what is known as the Great Exchange—and it's the most fabulous news in the Bible! Christ took upon Himself our sin and death, that we might receive His abundant, eternal life. The Son of God gave Himself for humanity, "the just for the unjust; the innocent for the guilty," [3] that we might *live*! The realization has a vitalizing effect on the soul, wrenching us out of our habitual self-absorption and reversing our otherwise inevitable falling away from God. By beholding this marvel of the cross we become changed: as we *identify* with Christ's great sacrifice in our behalf, by faith we see ourselves crucified with Him, and with Him are raised to newness of life. (See Galatians 2:20.)

The miraculous outcome of this new birth is that we who were once rebellious breakers of the Law of Life and Love, become, through God's indwelling Spirit, cooperative law *keepers,* as we willingly internalize the divine principles we had previously opposed:

> "The heart is brought into harmony with God, as it is brought into accord with His law. When this mighty change has taken place in the sinner, he has passed from death unto life; from sin unto holiness, from transgression and rebellion to obedience and loyalty. The old life of alienation from God has ended; the new life of reconciliation, of faith and love, has begun. Then 'the righteousness of the law' will 'be fulfilled in us, who walk not after the flesh, but after the Spirit.' "[4]

The glorious effect of Calvary is to deepen the conviction of sin experienced at Sinai, while at the same time providing a remedy for it. At the cross, we stand condemned by God's uncompromising purity, while our rebellious hearts are melted into submission by His unconditional love. "In the light that streams from Calvary the attributes of God which had filled us with fear and awe appear beautiful and attractive. Mercy, tenderness, and parental love are seen to blend with holiness, justice, and power." [5]

God has promised that as we reverently and appreciatively behold the Source of our salvation and what He has endured in our behalf—and at our hands—revival will come, as surely as a parched traveler is refreshed by the pure waters of a flowing fountain:

"And I will pour out on the house of David and the inhabitants of Jerusalem a spirit of grace and supplication. They will look on me, the one they have pierced, and they will mourn for him as one mourns for an only child, and grieve bitterly for him as one grieves for a firstborn son. ... On that day a fountain will be opened to the house of David and the inhabitants of Jerusalem, to cleanse them from sin and impurity" (Zechariah 12:10, 13:1, NIV).

As we drink deeply and continuously of this refreshing, purifying fountain, our spirits will be invigorated. We will be empowered to become more and more like our Savior, and to share His saving love with others. This is the essence of true revival, the only ground upon which it can be established and the lifeblood that sustains it—Christ our Righteousness.

Endnotes

1. C.S. Lewis, *The Problem of Pain* (New York: HarperCollins Publishers, 2001), p. 71.

2. Ellen G. White, *The Desire of Ages*, p. 25.

3. Ellen G. White, *Testimonies to the Church*, Volume 4, p. 251.

4. Ellen G. White, *The Great Controversy*, p. 468.

5. *Ibid.* p. 652.

Christ Our Righteousness

Chapter Four
A Love That Gives Itself Away

> *"Nowhere else is there to be found a revelation of Agape comparable to that in the death of Jesus on the Cross. ... It testifies that it is a love that gives itself away, that sacrifices itself, even to the uttermost."*
> —Anders Nygren, *Agape and Eros*[1]

Perhaps he didn't know she was a harlot when he married her. Perhaps she hadn't yet tapped into that primal, seductive part of herself, and how she could best exploit it. In any case, Hosea entrusted all the ardor and devotion of his youthful love to the daughter of Diblaim, and took her to be his wife. At first things went well enough. But after the birth of their first child, it all began to go drastically wrong—he couldn't know for sure whether the second child was his, and the third one clearly was not, which explains his enigmatic name: "Not-My-People" (Hosea 1:9). The gossip and the glances became cruel and cutting, and the lavish gifts and promises of her "lovers" bewitched her, until his faithless wife felt both driven and lured away from the only man who truly loved her, and the children who desperately needed her.[2]

So their marriage unraveled, and Gomer set up housekeeping in a virtual palace that became a monument to her adultery. Her pantry was well stocked with the finest bread and wine, with corn and olive oil. Her bed was luxuriously draped in the most exquisite linen; she decked herself lavishly with earrings and jewels, all of which served to rub the salt of rejection ever more deeply into the wounded heart of her jilted husband, who loved her still.

Then, predictably, the inevitable incursions of age stole upon this once radiant beauty. The finest Egyptian cosmetics could no longer disguise the furrowing eyes and pallid lips; her paramours' "love" faded into disinterest, then contempt. Wasted and abandoned, she hocked her fine linen and her glittering jewelry; she indebted herself to her creditors until they flung her on the auction block and sold her into slavery, like so much human refuse. It was then, when she was at her most desperate and undesirable, that her abandoned husband reclaimed her as his own. For "fifteen shekels of silver, and one and one-half homers of barley"—the price of a common maidservant—Hosea redeemed and reinstated the wife who had wrung and broken his heart (Hosea 3:2). And in so doing, he mirrored the love of God for a nation, and a world, that had done precisely that to Him.

The love of God for a world that did not love Him is the meta-narrative of the Bible. It's the golden thread that runs through every deliverance, every judgment, every prophetic plaint. And it reaches its zenith in the fulfillment of all the foreshadowing: At the cross, God conclusively and eternally demonstrated to the entire universe that He is love, and that His love is of a character that is foreign to our dark world. *Agape*, as the New Testament writers called it in the Greek, is a love that stands in stark contrast to the fickle, fragile, self-serving imitation we're so prone to mistake for the real thing. In the story of Hosea and Gomer, which so graphically prefigures the cross, we can discern the distinctive hallmarks of this otherworldly love:

1. ***Self-existent and proactive, agape reaches out of its fullness and takes the initiative in loving the other.*** Because it is

an overflowing fountain that continually replenishes itself, *agape* is not primed by the goodness or lovability of its object. Therefore, it is free to love even its enemies, as Paul has marveled: "God demonstrates His own love toward us, in that while we were still sinners, [enemies, vs. 10] Christ died for us" (Romans 5:8). In fact, the more needy the object, the more insistently God seeks it out, and the more determinedly He desires to pour His healing balm into the sin-sick soul.

Like Hosea seeking his broken wife, God sought us out when we were damaged goods. When the devil had used us up and discarded us as so much refuse, God pressed His way to the auction block and redeemed us—not "with corruptible things, like silver or gold … but with the precious blood of Christ" (1 Peter 1:18, 19). The Good Shepherd didn't wait for His one lost sheep to seek for Him; He eagerly abandoned the glories of heaven to descend to our dark world, "to seek and to save that which was lost" (Luke 19:10).

2. **Not only is agape intrinsically motivated to give of its fullness, it empties itself utterly for its beloved.** When Hosea redeemed his fallen bride, it cost him more than fifteen shekels of silver—it cost him his heart. He learned from painful experience that "to love at all is to be vulnerable. Love anything, and your heart will certainly be wrung and possibly be broken."[3] Such pain Jesus knew intimately, as His "heart was wrung with grief" at the "ingratitude and cruelty of those He had come to save,"[4] and as He ultimately, literally "died of a broken heart."[5]

Philippians 2:6–8 traces the steps that Jesus took in emptying Himself for our sakes:

"Who, being in the form of God, thought it not robbery to be equal with God: But made himself of no reputation, and took upon him the form of a servant, and was made in the likeness of men: And being found in fashion as a man, he humbled himself, and became obedient unto death, even the death of the cross."

Such a notion is absolutely foreign to humanism or paganism! God Himself, the Source and Sustainer of *everything*, became human and made Himself *nothing*, which is the literal meaning of "no reputation." He subjected His sensitive soul to the cruelest, most ignominious treatment that satanically inspired humanity could heap upon Him, and died the equivalent of our hopeless, god-forsaken "second death." Yet even as He "poured out His soul unto death," He became for us a "fountain of water springing up into everlasting life" (Isaiah 53:12; John 4:14).

3. *Agape gives itself utterly for its beloved, that it may elevate her to its level.* Though Hosea redeemed his wife for the price of a common maidservant, he didn't treat her as such. He reinstated her to her previous position, fully reinvesting her with the privileges and prerogatives of marriage. Just so, when God pursued His adulterous "wife" Israel, He promised that, when she should return to Him, "'It shall be, in that day ... that you will call Me "My *Husband*," and no longer call Me "My Master"'"—as her false gods, or "lovers," had demanded she do (Hosea 2:16).

Agape is able to accomplish this elevation of those it loves because it miraculously transforms them in the process of their receiving it. It accepts us as we *are*, even as it envisions and works to bring about what we *can be*, in Christ—and thank God that it's so. For "to ask that God's love should be content with us as we are is to ask that God should cease to be God: because

He is what He is, His love must, in the nature of things, be impeded and repelled by certain stains in our present character, and because He already loves us He must labour to make us lovable."[6]

So Christ pours His pure, principled, creative *agape* earthward that it may continually lift His people heavenward, that at the end of all things He may invite His victorious bride, "Sit with Me on My throne, as I also overcame and sat down with my Father on His throne" (Revelation 3:21).

4. *"Agape never fails"* (1 Corinthians 13:8). The story of Hosea and Gomer would have had quite a different ending if Hosea's love had withered under the ravages and the tedium of time. But because it was drawn from God's inexhaustible spring, it stood the test. Only divinely inspired *agape* "bears all things, believes all things, hopes all things, endures all things" (1 Corinthians 13:7). Ever hopeful, ever faithful, "many waters cannot quench" this "love, neither can the floods drown it" (Song of Solomon 8:7). It is a tenacious, "everlasting love" that, against all odds, believes in the best possible outcome, while doing everything in its power to bring it about (Jeremiah 31:3).

It's enough to make us exclaim with the apostle John: "Behold what manner of love the Father has bestowed on us!" (1 John 3:1). The human mind can never conjure such a love; the carnal mind can never comprehend it. It is a divine innovation imported into our dark world from the luminous center of the universe, at God's infinite expense. Destitute beggars all, we can only admit our never-ending need of it. For "only by love is love awakened"—and it is awakening that we so desperately need.[7]

Endnotes

1. Anders Nygren, *Agape and Eros* (Chicago: University of Chicago Press, 1982), p. 118.

2. See *The Seventh-day Adventist Bible Commentary*, Volume 4, pp. 888–896; if the story of Hosea's relationship with his adulterous wife, as recounted in chapters 1–3, is to be taken literally, and there is no contextual indication that it should not be, his prophetic commentary on Israel would seem to have been derived from his own personal, painful experience.

3. C.S. Lewis, *The Four Loves* (Orlando, FL: Harcourt Brace & Company, 1988), p. 121.

4. Ellen G. White, *Spirit of Prophecy*, Volume 3, p. 83.

5. Ellen G. White, *The Desire of Ages*, p. 772.

6. C.S. Lewis, *The Problem of Pain* (New York: HarperCollins Publishers, 2001), p. 41.

7. *The Desire of Ages*, p. 22.

Chapter Five
Amazing Grace!

*"In the matchless gift of His Son, God has encircled
the whole world with an atmosphere of grace as real
as the air which circulates around the globe."*
　　　　　　　　　—Ellen G. White, *Steps to Christ*[1]

The fierce north Atlantic gale had beaten and battered *The
Greyhound* for 11 grueling days. As rapidly as the bone-
weary sailors pumped the swirling seawater out, it surged
back in through the splintering hull. Sailor John Newton, too
exhausted to man the pumps, had been lashed to the helm to
hold the crippled ship to its course. From noon until midnight,
the ship's wheel thrust him about like a puppet as he fought to
hold it steady. Caught between nauseating fatigue and abject
terror, he was helpless to fend off the fragmented images of a
wasted life that filtered up to haunt him.

Having lost his devout mother at an early age, Newton was
taken to sea when he was 11 by his sea captain father. For the
next 12 years, he abandoned himself to a life of such vulgar and
utter debauchery that he shocked even his crusty fellow sailors.
At 19, he was impressed into service on a British warship but
found the conditions so miserable that he deserted, for which
he was publicly flogged and demoted. Transferred to a slaving
ship, he was captured off the coast of Sierra Leone by a tribal
chief who starved and brutally abused him. Eventually rescued

by a sea captain friend of his father's, "The Great Blasphemer," as he was known, promptly returned to slaving and adventuring, which is how he found himself strapped to a spinning ship's wheel in the boisterous north Atlantic, hanging between life and death.

As his memories rose up to mock him, conviction seized him like a vise, and he stood trembling before the judgment seat of God as truly as if he had been summoned by the trumpets of Sinai. Yet he dared to hope that God might forgive even a profligate wretch like him. Managing to find a New Testament, he hung his infant faith upon the words, "If ye then, being evil, know how to give good gifts unto your children: how much more shall your heavenly Father give the Holy Spirit to them that ask him?" (Luke 11:13, KJV). Ever after, John Newton regarded March 21, 1748, as the day on which he "was, by the rich mercy of our Lord and Saviour Jesus Christ, restored, pardoned, and appointed to preach the Gospel which he had long laboured to destroy."[2] It is to his conversion that we owe the world's most beloved hymn, "Amazing Grace."

Yet what is this amazing thing called "grace" that has power to transform a devoted libertine into a devout laborer for the gospel? While definitions abound, psychiatrist Gerald G. May has helpfully described it like this: "Grace is the active expression of God's love. God's love is the root of grace; grace itself is the dynamic flowering of this love; and the good things that result in life are the fruit of this divine process."[3]

All the good things that come to believers and nonbelievers alike—life, sustenance, the sweet entreaties of the Holy Spirit, and the ministry of angels—come because "God has encircled the whole world with an atmosphere of grace" that is "as real as the air which circulates around the globe." Suffusing our otherwise dark world with this radiant atmosphere of grace, God "makes His sun rise on the evil and on the good," "sends rain on the just and on the unjust," and pours out "every good and perfect gift" upon a prodigal humanity (Matthew 5:45;

James 1:17). And all of this He is able to do because "by [Christ's] death a restraint is removed from His love," enabling "His grace" to "act with unbounded efficiency."[4]

While God's posture toward this world has ever been one of magnanimous love, as we saw in our last chapter, our sin placed a restraint on His love. In order for God to maintain His integrity, upon which the stability of the universe rests, and at the same time reach out in blessing to sinful humanity, He had to do more than have warm feelings toward us. He had to deal with our sin. Because "the wages of sin is death"—both inherently and judicially—it can only be conclusively dealt with by being done away with (Romans 6:23). This Christ did, as he was "made ... to be sin for us" and died the equivalent of our eternal death (2 Corinthians 5:21). "By dying in our behalf He gave an equivalent for our debt. Thus He removed from God all charge of lessening the guilt of sin."[5]

At the cross, *agape* triumphed by both dealing with sin and letting the sinner free. So we become the privileged recipients of the flowering of God's love, as we bask in the life-giving atmosphere of His unmerited favor.[6] Thus, as Ellen White has so eloquently put it, "to the death of Christ we owe even this earthly life. The bread we eat is the purchase of His broken body. The water we drink is bought by His spilled blood. Never one, saint or sinner, eats his daily food, but he is nourished by the body and the blood of Christ. The cross of Calvary is stamped on every loaf. It is reflected in every water spring."[7]

Yet while grace flows "with unbounded efficiency" from God's magnanimous heart of love to our sinful world through the merits of Christ, only those who gain "access *by faith* into this grace" will be empowered to unwrap the free gift and fully experience its contents (Romans 5:2). As May has observed, "The alignment of our will with God's must happen at a heart level, through authentic choices of faith that are empowered by God,"[8] if we would receive *all* the treasures of grace that Christ desires to give us—including forgiveness from sin, peace with

God and our fellow beings, moral purity, emotional maturity, and ultimately, immortality.

When John Newton's eyes were finally opened to this marvelous truth of grace, it won his disaffected heart. If God had loved and sustained him so devotedly even while he persisted in rebellion against Him, had saved his wretched life, and borne the penalty of his perversity even before he'd asked for it, how could he not open his heart to receive of Christ's fullness and devote the rest of his life to Him? And so we continue to be both convicted and inspired by his heartfelt confession:

"Amazing grace! How sweet the sound
That saved a wretch like me!
I once was lost, but now am found;
Was blind, but now I see."

At the end of his long life of tireless ministry, his health rapidly failing, Newton succinctly summed up his world view, "My memory is nearly gone; but I remember two things: That I am a great sinner, and that Christ is a great Savior."

Upon these two vital truths revival is built. May God's grace enable us to experience them.

Endnotes

1. Ellen G. White, *Steps to Christ*, p. 68.

2. From his self-composed epitaph, as found in St. Mary Woolnoth church in London.

3. Gerald G. May, M.D., *Addiction and Grace* (New York: HarperCollins Publishers, 1988), p. 120.

4. Ellen G. White, *The Youth's Instructor*, December 16, 1897.

5. *Ibid.*

6. "When we had nothing to recommend us to God, Christ gave his life for us. With his long human arm he encircles the race, while with his divine arm he grasps the throne of the infinite. Thus finite man is united with the infinite God. The world, divorced from God by sin, has been restored to favor by the sacrifice of his Son. With his own

body the Saviour has bridged the gulf that sin has made." Ellen G. White, *General Conference Bulletin*, 1901.

7. Ellen G. White, *The Desire of Ages*, p. 660.

8. *Addiction and Grace*, p. 140.

Chapter Six
Made Like His Brethren

*"The humanity of the Son of God is everything to us.
It is the golden chain that binds our souls to Christ,
and through Christ to God. This is to be our study."*
—Ellen G. White, *Selected Messages, Book One* [1]

As he maneuvered his flock through the cool shadows of a southern Sinai wadi, Moses' attention was arrested by an otherworldly sight. Nestled among the tumbled granite and flowering acacias, a bramble bush [2] appeared to be burning, yet it was not consumed. Fearful, yet compelled by curiosity, he crept cautiously toward the spectacle until he was stopped by an authoritative Voice: " 'Take your sandals off your feet,' " it commanded, " 'for the place where you stand is holy ground' " (Exodus 3:5). Awestruck, Moses tremblingly complied. When the Voice continued, " 'I am the God of your father—the God of Abraham, the God of Isaac, and the God of Jacob,' Moses hid his face, for he was afraid to look upon God" (Verses 5, 6).

The paradox here is striking—the infinite God who made heaven and earth, who would soon after thunder from the pinnacle of Sinai, chose to introduce Himself to Israel's deliverer through the symbolism of a "lowly shrub, that seemingly had no attractions ... The all-merciful God shrouded His glory in a most humble type, that Moses could look upon it and live." [3]

33

It was a revelation to Moses, and to all who would come after, that God would find His greatest joy in veiling His glory in the lowly "body of our humiliation," "that He might draw near to sorrowful, tempted men" (Philippians 3:21, RV). [4]

So when the fullness of the time had come, Jesus, the "express image of [God's] person," who upheld "all things by the word of His power," drew near to our sorrowful, tempted race by consenting to be "born of the seed of David according to the flesh" (Hebrews 1:3; Romans 1:3). This means that when He said, "'Lo, I come … a body You have prepared for Me,'" the body to which He joined His divinity was just like the "lowly 'body of our humiliation.'" As Ellen White has explained:

> "It would have been an almost infinite humiliation for the Son of God to take man's nature, even when Adam stood in his innocence in Eden. But Jesus accepted humanity when the race had been weakened by four thousand years of sin. Like every child of Adam He accepted the results of the working of the great law of heredity. What these results were is shown in the history of His earthly ancestors. He came with such a heredity to share our sorrows and temptations, and to give us the example of a sinless life." [5]

This is the most comforting news in the Bible! The "High and Lofty One who inhabits eternity" subjected Himself to His own divinely established laws of heredity, and "became *flesh*"—*our* tempted, "sinful flesh"—that we need never again feel orphaned and alone in this inhospitable world (Isaiah 57:15; John 1:14; Romans 8:3). In Christ, we find the Friend "who was made like his brothers in every way," that He might stick closer to us even than a brother (Hebrews 2:17, NIV; see Proverbs 18:24). In Christ, we find a complete Savior who can both empathize with us in our spiritual struggles and empower us on to victory, because He "was in all points tempted as we are, yet without sin" (Hebrews 4:15).

Christ's assumption of our fallen nature carries weighty implications for every phase of His ministry. In terms of His humanity, it is what qualifies Him to be our Sacrifice, Example, and High Priest. Let's briefly examine these implications:

1. ***Christ our Sacrifice:*** "Inasmuch then as the children have partaken of flesh and blood, He Himself likewise shared in the same, that through death He might destroy him who had the power of death, that is, the devil, and release those who through fear of death were all their lifetime subject to bondage. For indeed He does not give aid to angels, but He does give aid to the seed of Abraham" (Hebrews 2:14–16).

In order to destroy the parasitic plant of sin, Christ had to enter the place where it resides and thoroughly uproot it. So He had to invest Himself in the reality, not just the resemblance, "of sinful flesh" in order to "condemn sin in the flesh" (See Romans 8:3). He condemned and destroyed sin where it thrives, by daily denying its incessant urges, by subjecting His opinions and preferences to the scrutiny of the Word and the Spirit, and by ultimately surrendering up the sinful flesh to "the death of the cross" (Philippians 2:8). Having "taste[d] death for everyone," Christ has rendered the second, god-forsaken death—hence our dread of it—unnecessary (Hebrews 2:9). He has truly stormed the gates of hell and spoiled the devil's dark domain of fear and bondage.

2. ***Christ our Example:*** While Christ is first and foremost our self-sacrificing Savior, He is secondarily our Example. And it is here that we must be careful to strike a biblical balance, to prevent us from falling into either of the twin traps of cheap grace or perfectionism. So we're assured, "Our Saviour took humanity, with all its liabilities. He took the nature

of man, with the possibility of yielding to temptation. We have nothing to bear which He has not endured."[6] Yet we're also cautioned, "You cannot equal the copy; but you can resemble it and, according to your [Spirit-assisted] ability, do likewise."[7]

Leroy Moore has wisely observed that, while Christ "was exactly like us in biological inheritance," He "was very unlike us in that sin had never infected His higher, spiritual faculties. From His conception the Holy Spirit directed His body every moment!"[8] This has not been the case for us who have an established track record of sin with all of its neuro-physiological implications. Still, our only solution is to look to Christ, who "came in just such flesh as ours, but with a mind that held its integrity against every temptation, against every inducement to sin—a mind that never consented to sin—no, never in the least conceivable shadow of a thought."[9]

3. **Christ our High Priest:** "Therefore, in all things He had to be made like His brethren, that He might be a merciful and faithful High Priest in things pertaining to God, to make propitiation [reconciliation] for the sins of the people. For in that He Himself has suffered, being tempted, He is able to aid those who are tempted" (Hebrews 2:17, 18). In His capacity as our High Priest, Christ "aids" His tempted people by inculcating us with His principles and transferring to us His heavenly attributes—imbuing us with His "mind." He reconciles us to God by subduing our wills and reconciling us to His selfless, righteous character.

Empathizing and identifying with us in our weakness, He is "not ashamed to call" us "brethren" (Hebrews 2:11). "For we do not have a High Priest who cannot sympathize with our weaknesses, but was in all points tempted as we are, yet without sin. Let us therefore come boldly to the throne of grace, that we may obtain mercy and find grace to help in time of need" (Hebrews 4:15).

What a complete Savior! When we wandered from God in Adam, He pursued us in Christ. Refusing to relinquish us to the devil, He shouldered responsibility for His erring creation and superseded Adam as the new head of the race. He *actually* became one with us by stepping into the stream of humanity and genetically linking Himself to us. He *experientially* became one with us by living out His life among us and identifying with our joys, our sorrows, even our guilt. He *representatively* became one with us by substituting His obedient life for our failed experiments with sin, dying the equivalent of our eternal death, and "bearing our human form before the Father's throne," [10] where He daily mediates in our behalf.

This is Christ our Righteousness, the Source of all true revival and the Inspiration for all lasting reformation. Having laid our foundation in Him, we are ready to consider our response to His saving initiative.

Endnotes

1. Ellen G. White, *Selected Messages, Book One*, p. 244.

2. The Hebrew *ceneh* literally means "a bramble;" some have taken this to be the *Dictamnus albus*, commonly called "burning bush," which emits lemon-peel scented, volatile, flammable vapors through secretor glands located mainly in its leaves and flowers.

3. Ellen G. White, *The Desire of Ages*, p. 23.

4. *Ibid.*

5. *Ibid.* p. 49.

6. *Ibid.* p. 117.

7. Ellen G. White, *Testimonies to the Church*, Volume 2, p. 169.

8. A. Leroy Moore, *Adventism in Conflict* (Hagerstown, MD: Review and Herald Publishing Association), p. 150.

9. A.T. Jones, *General Conference Bulletin*, 1895, p. 328.

10. Ellen G. White, *Steps to Christ*, p. 14.

Repentance and Confession

Chapter Seven
A Cautionary Lesson in How *Not* to Repent

> *"Or do you despise the riches of His goodness, forbearance, and longsuffering, not knowing that the goodness of God leads you to repentance?"*
>
> —Romans 2:4

I t was a rather incongruous sight: a strapping young Hercules of a man, splendidly handsome and a full head taller than any of his countrymen—hiding among the mountains of baggage like a frightened schoolboy. But on the day of his coronation, before he had become accustomed to the privileges and prerogatives of kingship, Saul was still "little in [his] own eyes" (1 Samuel 15:17). He was still spiritually sensitive and malleable, still responsive to the gentle pangs of conscience and the loving reproof of his peers.

It didn't take long for the sense of entitlement to set in. Two years after he responded to God's call, God tested him to see if he would place his full confidence in Him. With the massive Philistine war machine surging in on every side, Saul was to muster the Israelite militia at Gilgal and wait for Samuel, who would offer sacrifices in their behalf. As instructed, Saul waited seven days, but instead of "encouraging the people and inspiring confidence in God," he "indulged in unbelief and foreboding,"[1] which was as toxic as it was infectious. With his petrified troops bolting by the thousands into the caves and crannies, Saul summarily usurped the role of priest and, in full battle armor, slew the sacrificial animals himself and dared to offer them on God's altar.

Soon after, Samuel arrived and asked in disbelief, "'What have you done?'" (1 Samuel 13:11).

The self-justification was immediate: "When I saw that the men were scattering, and that you did not come at the set time, and that the Philistines were assembling at Micmash, I thought, 'Now the Philistines will come down against me ... and I have not sought the Lord's favor.' So I felt compelled to offer the burnt offering" (vs. 11, 12 NIV).

While Saul's behavior under fire might seem understandable from a humanistic perspective, it was an unacceptable breach of faith and good judgment for the intended dynastic progenitor of Israel. Blaming everyone and everything but his own impatience and unbelief, Saul demonstrated an aversion to accepting accountability that, if indulged, would totally unfit him for leadership, spiritual or otherwise. Yet even Samuel's severe censure couldn't bring him to his senses and any semblance of repentance.

Time served only to increase his penchant for rationalizing and deflecting responsibility. Still, God bore patiently with His erring monarch, and some years later gave Saul another prime opportunity to "learn the lesson of unquestioning faith ... and obedience."[2] Through Samuel, God instructed Saul to annihilate the Amalekites, who, through their persistent perversity, had exhausted their probation. Such an execution of retributive justice required that its object be "utterly destroyed,"[3] indicating that it was under the divine curse, the equivalent of the second death.[4] Yet "Saul and his army spared Agag and the best of the sheep and cattle, the fat calves and lambs—everything that was good. These they were unwilling to destroy completely, but everything that was despised and weak they totally destroyed" (1 Samuel 15:9, NIV).

When Samuel confronted him on his latest subversion of a divine directive, he was treated to the now familiar refrain of denial, rationalization, and blame, with the addition of a brazen lie: "'But I *have* obeyed the voice of the Lord, and gone on the mission on which the Lord sent me, and brought back Agag king of Amalek; I have *utterly destroyed* the Amalekites. But the *people* took of the plunder, sheep and oxen, the best of the things which should have been utterly destroyed, to sacrifice to the Lord your God in Gilgal'" (vs. 20, 21, italics added).

It was only when Samuel ominously pronounced, " 'Because you have rejected the word of the Lord, he has rejected you as king,' " that Saul apparently repented: "I have sinned," he confessed in an agony of fear. "I violated the Lord's command and your instructions. I was afraid of the people and so I gave in to them. Now I beg you, forgive my sin" (vs. 23–25 NIV).

Yet tragically, "it was not sorrow for sin, but fear of its penalty, that actuated the king of Israel ... If Saul had had true repentance, he would have made public confession of his sin."[5] But lacking any deep "conversion of purpose" or "abhorrence of evil,"[6] the best Saul could muster was a quasi-repentance that was nothing more than an admission of facts after he had been embarrassingly exposed. Such disingenuous, superficial repentance and confession, we are told, is "forced from the soul by an awful sense of condemnation and a fearful looking for of judgment. But such confessions cannot save the sinner."[7]

We are cautioned that we are not immune from the inclination to engage in such empty repentance. Like Saul, "There are many who fail to understand the true nature of repentance. Multitudes sorrow that they have sinned and even make an outward reformation because they fear that their wrongdoing will bring suffering upon themselves. But this is not repentance in the Bible sense. They lament the suffering rather than the sin."[8]

Lamenting his suffering rather than his sin, refusing to acknowledge that his own perverse choices were the cause of that suffering, Saul persisted in his unrepentant course until he became "little less than a madman."[9] He bullied his sons, tyrannized his subjects, blatantly disregarded divine directives, and blamed everyone else for his moral failures. His conscience hardened, his will habitually bent toward rebellion, his ambitions and affections decisively pitted against his Maker, he became a living testimony to the truth of the observation that "Every act of transgression, every neglect or rejection of the grace of Christ, is reacting upon yourself; it is hardening the heart, depraving the will, benumbing the understanding, and *not only making you less inclined to yield, but less capable of yielding*, to the tender pleading of God's Holy Spirit."[10]

Having become disinclined and virtually incapable of yielding to the God he had decidedly rejected, Saul, in a moment of crisis, sought solace from a witch (1 Samuel 28). Fully and finally ensnared by Satan, he was shortly thereafter slain by his own hand.

It's a cautionary lesson for every one of us, who, while perhaps not as temperamentally extreme as Saul, naturally share his aversion to personal accountability. True sons and daughters of our fallen parents, we pass the buck as naturally as we breathe. But if we would be revived from spiritual decline and death, we must relinquish the self-righteousness that sabotages repentance; we must surrender the rebellious spirit that is "'as the sin of witchcraft,'" and the "'stubbornness [that] is as iniquity and idolatry'" (1 Samuel 15:23).

God "is wooing by His tender love the hearts of His erring children. … All His promises, His warnings, are but the breathing of unutterable love."[11] If we reject His love, if we despise His "goodness, forbearance, and longsuffering," which alone can lead us to repentance, what means does He have left to reach our hearts?

Endnotes

1. Ellen G. White, *Patriarchs and Prophets*, p. 617.

2. *Ibid.*, p. 627.

3. According to Strong's Exhaustive Concordance, the Hebrew *charam* means to "seclude; specifically (by a ban) to devote to religious uses (especially destruction) ... make accursed, consecrate, (utterly) destroy, devote, forfeit ... utterly (slay, make away)."

4. While this seems a horrendously bloodthirsty act to us, we must remember that God sustained a unique relationship to theocratic Israel, through whom He executed judgment upon irredeemable people groups: "While [God] does not delight in vengeance, He will execute judgment upon the transgressors of His law. He is forced to do this, to preserve the inhabitants of the earth from utter depravity and ruin. In order to save some He must cut off those who have become hardened in sin." *Patriarchs and Prophets*, p. 628.

5. *Ibid.*, p. 631.

6. Ellen G. White, *Steps to Christ*, p. 23.

7. *Patriarchs and Prophets*, p. 498.

8. *Steps to Christ*, p. 23.

9. *Patriarchs and Prophets*, p. 663.

10. *Steps to Christ*, p. 33 (italics supplied).

11. *Ibid.*, p. 35.

Chapter Eight
Create in Me a Clean Heart

"The sacrifices of God are a broken spirit, A broken and a contrite heart—These, O God, You will not despise."

—Psalm 51:17

I n complete contrast to Saul, a larger-than-life action hero after the people's own heart, God established Israel's monarchy in David, "a man after *His* own heart" (1 Samuel 13:14, italics added). God could say this about David because, as the young shepherd contemplated His magnificent creation and magnanimous character, his heart resonated with God's heart, until they beat as one. Ardent, humble, teachable, David developed into the king who would represent the best and noblest of the Israelite monarchy.

Yet God has preserved, for our instruction, a detailed account of the stain that would come to characterize the moral nadir of David's kingship. Predictably, it came when he had arrived at the apex of his worldly success and popularity. Having "transformed a throne created by brutal military necessity into a glittering institution which combined religious sanction, oriental luxury and new standards of culture,"[1] David was assaulted by an enemy more treacherous than an attacking army. As "the subtle allurements of power and luxury" insinuated themselves into his life, they "were not without effect."[2] Gradually, David became intoxicated. "Instead of relying in humility upon the power of Jehovah, he began to trust to his own wisdom and might," and as "the spirit of self-confidence and self-exaltation" supplanted his habitual humility, it "prepared the way for David's fall."[3]

His fall consisted of a head-on collision with autocratic entitlement and sensual abandon in his infamous affair with Bathsheba, and quickly led to the murder of her husband, in a desperate attempt to cover-up what was a punishable-by-death crime. But while David thought he had covered his tracks, people inevitably began to talk, and the cause of God was dishonored. If the deceitful king would not make things right on his own, it was time for God to intervene.

He sent Nathan the prophet to confront David in such a way as to "engage the sympathies of the king ... arouse his conscience, and ... call from his lips the sentence of death upon himself."[4] The confrontation had the desired effect: "The prophet's rebuke touched the heart of David; conscience was aroused; his guilt appeared in all its enormity. His soul was bowed in penitence before God. With trembling lips he said, 'I have sinned against the Lord.' "[5]

While the language of David's confession was identical to that of Saul's, the motivation behind the words was vastly different. David did not "lament the suffering rather than the sin;"[6] he lamented the sin itself. "His repentance was sincere and deep. There was no effort to palliate his guilt; no desire to escape the judgment threatened. ... David saw the enormity of his transgression; he saw the defilement of his soul; he *loathed* his sin."[7]

Why did David "loathe" his sin? By what means was he able to experience such an otherworldly hatred for that which fallen humanity naturally loves? God had opened his spiritual eyes and enabled him to penetrate sin's veneer to the underlying reality. When he discerned Christ and Him crucified in consequence of his sin, he saw "the enormity of his transgression," and he *loathed* it:

"It is when we most fully comprehend the love of God that we best realize the sinfulness of sin. When we see the length of the chain that was let down for us, when we understand something of the infinite sacrifice that Christ has made in our behalf, the heart is melted with tenderness and contrition."[8]

His heart melted with tenderness and contrition, David desperately desired to be free of the sin that would cause the death of his beloved Lord. He wished never to repeat it. So he prayed, not only "for pardon ... but for purity of heart:"[9] "*Wash* me thoroughly from my iniquity, and *cleanse* me from my sin," he pleaded; "Create in me a *clean* heart, O God, and renew a steadfast spirit within me" (Psalm 51:2, 10, italics added). Discerning that God did not desire appeasement, but fellowship, David prayed, "You do not desire sacrifice, or else I would give it; You do not delight in burnt offering. The sacrifices of God are *a broken spirit, a broken and a contrite heart*; These, O God, You will not despise" (vs. 16, 17, italics added).

So truly sorry was David for his sin, so earnestly did he desire to vindicate His God, whose character he had so grossly misrepresented, and so anxious was he to spare others the heartache of following in his footsteps, that he did the unthinkable. In utter contrast to Saul, who had concealed his sin at all costs, David publicly confessed the sin that would have such far-reaching, public consequences. And he went so far as to incorporate his repentance and confession into the temple liturgy:

"In a sacred song to be sung in the public assemblies of his people, in the presence of the court—priests and judges, princes and men of war—and which would preserve to the latest generation the knowledge of his fall, the king

of Israel recounted his sin, his repentance, and
his hope of pardon through the mercy of God.
Instead of endeavoring to conceal his guilt he
desired that others might be instructed by the sad
history of his fall." [10]

Such thorough, radical repentance led to thorough, radical
reformation, such that "decided changes" were made, and
"everything offensive to God" was "put away." [11] Insofar as it
was within his power, David endeavored to make right what
he had made so terribly wrong. And while it might strike us as
a gospel oxymoron, He accepted God's magnanimous gift of
forgiveness even while forbidding himself to forget the sin that
had made it necessary. As he consciously kept his "sin … always
before" him, he maintained an awareness of his vulnerability,
and experienced an ever-deepening repentance that prevented
him from falling prey to it again (Psalm 51:3).

Far from being a dismal, depressive experience, David's
godly sorrow set him free from that which had oppressed his
soul and alienated him from God. Infinitely grateful, infinitely
humbled, he "was now more fully in harmony with God and in
sympathy with his fellow men than before he fell." [12]

The story of David's tragic fall and joyful restoration assures
us that there is no sin for which God has not provided repentance
and forgiveness. On the other hand, the remedy supplied testifies
to the costliness of the Gift. As we look to Calvary, if we don't
resist the drawing power of Christ's magnetic love, the question
will well up within us:

"What is sin, that it should require such a sacrifice
for the redemption of its victim? Was all this love,
all this suffering, all this humiliation, demanded,
that we might not perish, but have everlasting
life?" [13]

The answer is that sin is just that bad, and God is just that good. And if we don't resist, His goodness *will* lead us all the way to repentance and joyful reconciliation with Him.

Endnotes

1. Paul Johnson, *A History of the Jews* (New York: HarperCollins Publishers, 1987), p. 55.

2. Ellen G. White, *Patriarchs and Prophets*, p. 717.

3. *Ibid.*

4. *Ibid.*, pp. 720–721.

5. *Ibid.*, p. 722.

6. Ellen G. White, *Steps to Christ*, p. 23.

7. *Ibid.*, p. 24–25 (italics supplied).

8. *Ibid.*, p. 36.

9. *Ibid.*, p. 25.

10. *Patriarchs and Prophets*, p., 725; as per *Steps to Christ*, p. 38: "True confession is always of a specific character, and acknowledges particular sins. They may be of such a nature as to be brought before God only; they may be wrongs that should be confessed to individuals who have suffered injury through them; or they may be of a public character, and should then be as publicly confessed. But all confession should be definite and to the point, acknowledging the very sins of which you are guilty."

11. *Step to Christ*, p. 39.

12. *Patriarchs and Prophets*, p. 726. This is not to diminish the severity of his sin and its consequences, or to say that we should feel free to "sin, that grace may abound"—as Paul has objected, "God forbid" (Romans 6:1–2, KJV).

13. *Steps to Christ*, p. 27.

Chapter Nine
The Perfect Penitent

> *"No man is an island, entire of itself; every man is a piece of the continent, a part of the main … any man's death diminishes me, because I am involved in mankind; and therefore never send to know for whom the bell tolls; it tolls for thee."*
>
> —John Donne
> *Devotions upon Emergent Occasions [1624], no. 17*

As to the stories written in faces, he thought he had read them all—this wild man of the desert. He had studied the story of war etched into the stoic, chiseled features of mercenaries; he had seen the greed and love of ease folded into the refined features of publicans and princes; had marked the hopelessness and self-hatred harbored in the powdered countenances of prostitutes. And though they tried to hide it, he'd discerned the poisonous pride neatly tucked beneath the pretensions of the religious hypocrites, whom he rightly called "vipers." But never had he beheld a face so radiant with self-forgetful love, so utterly defined by peace and purity. But then, never before had he beheld Jesus.

Lost in worshipful awe, John barely noticed as Jesus stepped into the muddy waters of the Jordan, until the realization hit him like a thunderclap: this Holy Being was requesting baptism at his hands! Yet "how could he, a sinner, baptize the Sinless

One? And why should He who needed no repentance submit to a rite that was a confession of guilt to be washed away?"[1]

"I need to be baptized by *You*," John protested, "and are You coming to *me*?" (Matthew 3:14, italics added).

Jesus' reply was characteristically enigmatic: "Permit it to be so now, for thus it is fitting for us to fulfill all righteousness" (v. 14).

In what sense was Jesus fulfilling "all righteousness" by submitting to a baptism of repentance like a common sinner? Was He simply demonstrating the right method by which we should experience it, or was there something deeper at stake?

> "Christ came not confessing His own sins; but guilt was imputed to Him as the sinner's substitute. He came not to repent on His own account; but in behalf of the sinner. ... In this act He identified himself with His people as their representative and head. As their substitute, He takes upon Him their sins, numbering Himself with the transgressors, taking the steps the sinner is required to take, and doing the work the sinner must do."[2]

Jesus "filled righteousness full" by identifying with us to the point of taking "the necessary steps in repentance, conversion, and faith in behalf of the human race," and then seeking out "John to be baptized of him in Jordan," as the prototypical, Perfect Penitent.[3] When we experience godly sorrow for our sinfulness, we are partaking of a repentance that "Christ our Righteousness" has already wrought out and perfected in our behalf. The road to righteousness has been paved by his loving footsteps, and we can't travel anywhere on it that He has not traveled first.

This means that Jesus did not impassively go through the motions of repentance and conversion, like a seasoned actor in a passion play. In absolute solidarity with us, He *actually* experienced the overwhelming self-revulsion and heartbreaking grief of profound repentance. He empathized with every tempted, sorrowful child of Adam and Eve to the point of virtually *being* us:

> "As one with us, He must bear the burden of our guilt and woe. The Sinless One must *feel* the shame of sin. The peace lover must dwell with strife, the truth must abide with falsehood, purity with vileness. Every sin, every discord, every defiling lust that transgression had brought, was torture to His spirit."[4]

As Immanuel, God with us, Jesus felt to the depths of His being both holy sorrow for our sin and infinite pity for our sinfulness. As our hearts are melted by this comforting, catalyzing truth, an amazing thing happens—we are first transformed into grateful recipients, then into earnest imitators. Our lives become a never-ending journey into "continual repentance and humility,"[5] and our circle of repentance grows ever larger to take in all who are within our sphere. In imitation of our empathetic High Priest, we grow up into a mature "holy priesthood," able to "offer up spiritual sacrifices acceptable to God through Jesus Christ" (1 Peter 2:5). We become, in effect, priestly purveyors of repentance:

> "As we see souls out of Christ, we are to put ourselves in their place, and in their behalf feel repentance before God, resting not until we bring them to repentance. If we do everything we can for them, and yet they do not repent, the sin lies at their door; but we are still to feel sorrow of heart because of their condition, showing them how to repent, and trying to lead them step by step to Jesus Christ."[6]

While our repentance in behalf of others can never be meritorious, as was Christ's, it is an effective and necessary catalyst for revival. How so? We humans are social creatures; like so many thirsty sponges, we absorb the substance of our social environment by osmosis. We are devastated by rejection and encouraged by affirmation, which means that when our fellow beings care enough about us to empathetically identify with us, our hearts are deeply touched.

Yet such repentant intercession penetrates to a level that is even deeper than that of emotional response: It effectively strikes at the *foundation* of the devil's preeminent strategy of "divide and conquer" by reconciling what sin has alienated, by reconstituting what it has shattered. It "works" at the level of principle, by restoring in fallen humanity the loving, selfless image of God, against which all the "principalities and powers" of Satan are powerless to stand (Ephesians 3:10).

The Bible is replete with examples of the vital role such priestly penitence has played in facilitating church-wide repentance, revival and reformation:

- Though personally innocent of any wrongdoing, when Ezra was confronted with the perversity of his fellow Israelites, he confessed, "*Our* iniquities have risen higher than our heads, and *our* guilt has grown up to the heavens. Since the days of our fathers to this day *we* have been very guilty"—which helped to instigate a thorough revival and "wonderful reformation" [7] (Ezra 9:6, 7, italics added).

- The spotless Daniel, "greatly beloved" of heaven, "identified himself fully with those who had fallen short of the divine purpose, confessing their sins as his own," [8] as he prayed: "O Lord, to us belongs shame of face, to our kings, our princes, and our fathers, because *we* have sinned against You … *we* have rebelled … *we* have done wickedly!" (Daniel 9:8, 9, 15, italics added). His repentant intercession helped to facilitate Judah's return to their homeland following their 70-year Babylonian exile.

- Moses, who was "more humble than anyone else on the face of the earth" (Numbers 12:8 NIV), so identified with his people's predicament in consequence of the golden calf debacle, that "he desired his name to be blotted out [of the book of life] with theirs," rather than live forever without them—illustrating "the mediation of Christ for sinful men."[9] His priestly repentance in their behalf helped to catalyze their own repentance and gradual reformation.

Through these examples and others, God encourages us to believe that, not only is it *possible* for faulty human beings to follow in the humble footsteps of the Perfect Penitent, it is *necessary* if we would help to awaken one another from our sin-drugged stupor. As we experience an ever- deepening sense of sorrow for our sinfulness, and corresponding reliance on Christ's righteousness, we can become bridges of repentance and reconciliation. We can advocate for one another as interdependent members of a whole that is greater than the sum of its parts, and help to facilitate a groundswell of latter rain revival that will continue to surge until it finds its glorious crescendo in the Second Coming of Christ.

Endnotes

1. Ellen G. White, *The Desire of Ages*, p. 110.

2. Ellen G. White, *Spirit of Prophecy*, Volume 2, p. 59.

3. Ellen G. White, *General Conference Bulletin*, 1901, p. 36.

4. *The Desire of Ages*, p. 111 (italics added).

5. *Seventh-day Adventist Bible Commentary*, Volume 7, p. 959 (MS 92, 1901).

6. *Ibid.*, p. 960 (MS 92, 1901).

7. Ellen G. White, *Prophets and Kings*, p. 622; as discussed in Chapter 1.

8. *Ibid.*, p. 555.

9. Ellen G. White, *Patriarchs and Prophets*, p. 326.

Faith and Acceptance

Chapter Ten
The Soul of Consecration

*"Consecration means dedication to God. It occurs
when we claim our deepest desire for God, beneath,
above, and beyond all other things."*
—Gerald G. May, M.D.
Addiction and Grace [1]

Addiction—how well she knew its siren song, how impotent she was to resist it. How intimately acquainted she was with the self-loathing that attaches like a parasite to the broken promises to get free, to the will that has become as weak as still water. Having surrendered her will up to seven devils, who had systematically taken possession of her thoughts and nerves until they ruled her, Mary hung helplessly in their iron grip, seducing as she had been seduced, exploiting as she had been exploited.

Even as she had mastered this oldest of professions, it had sucked her dry. The lavish gifts of her "patrons" couldn't compensate for the vitality they had siphoned from her, as they'd warmed themselves with the "calories" that her waning youth gave off "as a cooling pot gives off heat." [2] Now she had nothing left to give, yet she was compelled to give it, and compelled to try to fill the vacuum with something she could never seem to get, no matter how desperately she reached for it.

How had it come to this? Mary tried to trace the tangled strands of sin, but they had meshed and intersected until they had become a convoluted web of debased sensuality, shame, and galling bitterness. God alone saw and marked the hot tears that fell on her pillow as the morning sun unfailingly found her alone—devastatingly alone.

Then came the day God walked into her wreck of a life, and with tears as hot and heartfelt as her own, prayed for this fallen daughter of Abraham. She sensed, for the first time, her incredible worth. She saw it in His face so radiant with warm acceptance, felt it in the tenderness of His regard, heard it in His agonized intercession. "Seven times she ... heard His rebuke of the demons that controlled her heart and mind." Seven times "she ... heard His strong cries to the Father in her behalf." [3]

Yet she struggled to believe that Jesus could deliver her from the bondage she had tried so desperately to escape. She struggled, perhaps even more, to know whether she really *wanted* to be free, as her habitually mixed motivations kept her in a state of self-defeating ambivalence. It was a painful, protracted process, but as Jesus patiently prayed for and encouraged her, Mary began to see where her battle with sin and addiction centered—she needed desperately to understand "the true force of the *will*" [4]:

> "This is the governing power in the nature of man,
> the power of decision, or of *choice*. Everything
> depends on the right action of the will. The
> power of choice God has given to men; it is theirs
> to exercise. You cannot change your heart, you
> cannot of yourself give to God its affections; but
> you can *choose* to serve Him. You can give Him
> your *will*; He will then work in you to will and to
> do according to *His* good pleasure." [5]

Nearly suffocated by the heavy hand of demonic oppression, the tiny smoking flax of *freedom of choice* still smoldered within Mary's breast—God had made sure of it. And as she tentatively placed that smoking ember into Jesus' capable hands, He stoked it with His grace and love until it grew into an indomitable determination to be *free. Free* from the compulsion to engage in the soul-destroying practices that had brought her to the brink of ruin. *Free* from the bitterness that burned like acid when she thought of the man—a respected church leader, no less—who had seduced away her innocence and self-respect.

As Jesus prayed for Mary, the overwhelming awareness of the wretched failure she envisioned herself to be receded from her consciousness, as she caught His shining faith-vision of the person she *could be* in Him. Choosing *His* reality, she began to be transformed into it, until the day came when Mary knew she had been *set free.*

Her gratitude toward her deliverer knew no bounds! *Jesus* was the light of her life, the incarnate desire of her heart, the devoted husband and best friend she had always longed for. He was the ardent lover of her soul, her shining champion! Her complete surrender to Him of her will and affections came as naturally as a dependent flower turns toward the life-giving sun. Mary had discovered the secret of consecration:

> "When Christ dwells in the heart, the soul will be so filled with His love, with the joy of communion with Him, that it will cleave to Him; and in the contemplation of Him, self will be forgotten. Love to Christ will be the spring of action. Those who feel the constraining love of God, do not ask how little may be given to meet the requirements of God; they do not ask for the lowest standard, but aim at perfect conformity to the will of their Redeemer. With earnest desire they yield all and manifest an interest proportionate to the value of the object which they seek."[6]

It would never have occurred to Mary to ask "how little" she might give to meet God's "requirements." Constrained by love for Him who had so magnanimously loved her, Mary gave herself to Jesus with every fiber of her being. And in a love gift that cost every cent of her substance, Mary demonstrated her pure devotion in a way that would, to the end of time, epitomize the spirit of selfless consecration, and mirror the sacrificial love of Christ.

Hearing Jesus speak of His approaching death, Mary's grateful heart was filled with grief, and she longed to honor Him in some tangible way. Eagerly, she lavished "more than a year's wages" on "an alabaster jar of very expensive perfume" with which to anoint His precious body (Mark 14:3, 5 NIV). Lovingly, she kept the jar tucked into the folds of her clothing, next to her grateful, grieving heart, as she awaited the time when it would be needed. At a banquet one evening, as she characteristically sat at Jesus' feet catching every word that fell from His lips, Mary heard the whispered assertion that He would soon be crowned king. "Her grief was turned to joy, and she was eager to be first in honoring her Lord."[7]

Drawing the precious flask from beneath her heart, she silently broke it open and, in worshipful adoration, anointed Jesus' sacred head with the fragrant perfume, then fell weeping at His feet. Her act of pure devotion had been meant for His benefit only, but "the ointment filled the room with its fragrance, and published her act to all present."[8] Scandalized that Jesus would publicly submit to the advances of such a "sinner," and vexed by the prodigality of Mary's gift, the entire company heaped coals of reproach upon the now cowering woman, who had nothing to say in her defense.

> "Mary knew not the full significance of her deed of love. She could not answer her accusers. She could not explain why she had chosen that occasion for anointing Jesus. The Holy Spirit had planned for her, and she had obeyed His promptings. Inspiration stoops to give no reason. An unseen

presence, it speaks to mind and soul, and moves the heart to action. It is its own justification."[9]

Her Champion, as ever, came to her rescue. "Leave her alone!" He commanded; "Why are you bothering her? She has done a *beautiful* thing to me" (Mark 14:6 NIV, italics added). Then "Christ told Mary the meaning of her act."[10] "She has done what she could," He explained; "She has come beforehand to anoint My body for burial. Assuredly, I say to you, wherever this gospel is preached in the whole world, what this woman has done will also be told as a memorial to her" (Mark 14:8, 9).

So it has been. Mary's magnanimous act of devotion, "an earnest of the love that would be [Christ's] from His redeemed ones forever,"[11] has fittingly come to represent the very essence of consecration. It is a reflection of the consecration of Christ, who willingly and extravagantly gave His body to be broken that we might be made whole; who "loved us and gave himself up for us as a fragrant offering and sacrifice to God" (Ephesians 5:2 NIV).

Redolent with the righteousness of Christ, Mary's broken bottle will forever speak to us of the abundant forgiveness of a Savior who reached into our deepest hell to rescue us, and the astonishing power of a broken, yielded, consecrated heart.

Endnotes

1. Gerald G. May, M.D., *Addiction and Grace*, p. 149.

2. F. Scott Fitzgerald, *This Side of Paradise*, p. 258.

3. Ellen G. White, *The Desire of Ages*, p. 568.

4. Ellen G. White, *Steps to Christ*, p. 47 (italics supplied).

5. *Ibid.* (italics supplied).

6. *Ibid.*, pp. 44–45.

7. *The Desire of Ages*, p. 559.

8. *Ibid.*

9. *Ibid.*, p. 560.

10. *Ibid.*

11. *Ibid.*

Chapter Eleven
Faith That Works by Love

> *"Where there is not only a belief in God's word, but a submission of the will to Him; where the heart is yielded to Him, the affections fixed upon Him, there is faith—faith that works by love and purifies the soul. Through this faith the heart is renewed in the image of God."*
>
> —Ellen G. White *Steps to Christ* [1]

There is a surprising and wonderfully winsome postscript to the story of Mary and her broken bottle—a postscript that only God could write. And it concerns a heart so hardened by pride that only the surprisingly winsome love of God could soften and subdue it. This heart belonged to a certain "Simon the leper," so-called because, while he had been rendered a religious and social pariah by the dreaded disease, he had been graciously healed by Jesus. Grateful, but hedging his bets, Simon became a follower of the young Nazarene—from a socially and intellectually safe distance. While he entertained a nominal "faith" in Jesus as a teacher, he couldn't quite bring himself to accept Him as his Savior.

Still, Simon was thankful that Jesus had saved him from a living death, and in his honor held the feast at which Mary had so scandalously broken all the rules of banquet etiquette. While it was Judas who loudly raked her over the coals for "wasting" a year's wages on the Savior of the world, it was Simon who surreptitiously thought to himself, "This man, if He were a prophet, would know who and what manner of woman this is who is touching Him, for she is a *sinner*" (Luke 7:39, italics added). And this is where the plot, as they say, thickens.

Simon did indeed know—intimately so—that Mary had been a sinner. For Simon the Pharisee was the one who "had led into sin the woman he now despised. She had been deeply wronged by him."[2] As he watched those lips, with whose warmth he was so familiar, tenderly kiss the feet of Jesus; as he felt, more than saw, the long, silken hair cascade around her face and His feet, mingling with her now-perfumed tears, Simon imploded into a cauldron of hypocritical outrage. *How could any self-respecting man submit to the attentions of such a woman in public?* he mutely seethed. *And how could any man receive such attentions without sinning in response?*

Yet while the cagey Simon "thought himself reading his Guest, his Guest had been reading him."[3] Jesus "knew the circumstances that had shaped [Mary's] life;"[4] He knew who had been the predator and who had been the prey. Jesus did not treat Mary as Simon would have, had he been given the chance. Neither did He treat the far more guilty Simon as he deserved: "God's Son must act in God's way, with compassion, tenderness, and mercy."[5] So as Nathan had done with David, Jesus kindly yet skillfully nailed Simon with a parable that "threw upon His host the burden of pronouncing sentence upon himself."[6]

"Simon," He began, "I have something to say to you."

"Tell me, teacher," Simon casually replied, feigning composure he didn't feel.

"There was a certain creditor who had two debtors. One owed five hundred denarii, and the other fifty. And when they had nothing with which to repay, he freely forgave them both. Tell Me, therefore, which of them will love him more?"

Stroking his manicured beard, Simon carefully replied, "I *suppose* the one whom he forgave more."

Having lovingly caught His prey in the conviction trap, Jesus quietly concluded, "You have rightly judged" (Luke 7:40–43).

Simon was astonished! Gradually it dawned on him that, not only was Jesus "a prophet," He was much more. As Prophet, Priest, and Savior, Jesus had discerned his twin sins of predatory sensuality and self-righteousness, led him to pronounce himself guilty, and "freely" forgiven him—all in one fell swoop! At first seized by shame, Simon was subsequently filled with gratitude that Jesus had dealt so delicately with him in the presence of his guests. While "stern denunciation would have hardened Simon against repentance," Christ's "patient admonition convinced him of his error" [7] and won his pharisaical heart. His tender love had accomplished what nothing else could do: It awakened within Simon saving, transforming faith.

While Simon had considered himself a believer in Jesus, his "faith" had simply been an intellectual assent to the superior logic of Christ's arguments, and a superficial appreciation of His preeminent power. "Even the demons" possess such fact-oriented belief "and tremble"—yet are not converted (James 2:19). So Simon's "character was not transformed; his principles were unchanged." [8] Such nominal "faith," when put to the test, is actually hostile to Jesus' character and mission, as Simon demonstrated in his reaction to Jesus' gracious treatment of Mary. But when Simon realized that *he* was the undeserving recipient of Christ's gracious love, he saw his superficial belief for what it was. Genuine saving "faith that works by *love*" was energized into action, and "the proud Pharisee became a lowly, self-sacrificing disciple." [9]

It would perhaps be helpful to pause at this point, and ask the age-old question: What, then, is this thing called *faith*? Is it a mysterious, magical *something* that resides in some indefinable spiritual "center" within us? Is it something that God injects into us at the moment that we need it? Or could it be that "we cannot pin down where true faith comes from. We can truthfully say it comes from God, for God empowers our faith. But we can just as truthfully say it comes from ourselves, for it represents absolute human freedom. Or we can say ... that it comes from a mysterious coinherence of grace and will."[10]

Faith is fanned into life by grace, the "active expression" of God's love[11]—but it will never see the light of day without our sovereign consent. Neither all God's doing nor all our doing, yet all of *both*, "Saving faith is a *transaction* by which those who receive Christ join themselves in covenant relation with God."[12] It is a happy marriage of God's saving initiative with nothing less than every fiber of our being—our intellect and our affections, our willingness to both trust and risk, to appreciate and to persevere. As Herbert Douglass has helpfully explained, "Faith is simply the whole person saying '*Yes*' to God."[13] And as Ellen White has summed it up: "Genuine faith is *life*."[14]

Just as Simon entered into this life of faith—by yielding to Christ's character of love—so do we. And as we enter into it, so we are to live it, day by day:

> "By *faith* you became Christ's, and by faith you are to grow up in Him—by giving and taking. You are to *give* all—your heart, your will, your service—give yourself to Him to obey all His requirements; and you must *take* all—Christ, the fullness of all blessing, to abide in your heart, to be your strength, your righteousness, your everlasting helper—to give you power to obey."[15]

Birth begins life, and life is a continuation of birth. As we were *born* into Christ, so we *abide* in Him by faith—by both passively surrendering, and actively committing, ourselves to His care. As we daily behold His gracious character in His Word and His interactions with us, the love that awakened faith will work its way into our warp and woof until we freely extend it to others, in the process becoming obedient "doers of [God's] law," for "love is the fulfillment of the law" (Romans 2:13; 13:10). As John Wesley has so beautifully described it:

"Faith, then, was originally designed of God to re-establish the law of love. ... It is the grand means of restoring that holy love wherein man was originally created. It follows, that although faith is of no value in itself, (as neither is any other means whatsoever), yet as it leads to that end, the establishing anew the law of love in our hearts; and as, in the present state of things, it is the only means under heaven for effecting it; it is on that account an unspeakable blessing to man, and of unspeakable value before God."[16]

This is the goal of revival: that the faith that works by love will ultimately work to reestablish the law of love in our hearts. It "works" for profligate prostitutes, it works for hypocritical Pharisees. As we behold and partake of Christ's gracious character, it will work for, in, and through *us*—we have His Word on it.

Endnotes

1. Ellen G. White, *Steps to Christ*, p. 63.

2. Ellen G. White, *The Desire of Ages*, p. 566.

3. *Ibid.*, p. 567.

4. *Ibid.*, p. 568.

5. *Ibid.*, p. 566.

6. *Ibid.*

7. *Ibid.*, pp. 567–568.

8. *Ibid.*, p. 557.

9. *Ibid.*, p. 568.

10. Gerald G. May, *Addiction and Grace* (New York: HarperCollins Publishers, 1988), p. 132. Note: Coinherence means that both elements—grace and will—together constitute the essential "substance" or character of faith.

11. *Ibid.*, p. 120.

12. *The Desire of Ages*, p. 347 (italics added).

13. Herbert E. Douglass, *Should We Ever Say, "I Am Saved"?* (Nampa, ID: Pacific Press Publishing Association, 2003), p. 56 (italics added).

14. *Ibid.* (italics added).

15. *Steps to Christ*, p. 70 (italics in original).

16. John Wesley, as quoted in *Should We Ever Say, "I Am Saved"?*, p. 71.

Chapter Twelve
The Key in the Hand of Faith

"Prayer is the key in the hand of faith to unlock heaven's storehouse, where are treasured the boundless resources of Omnipotence."
—Ellen G. White *Steps to Christ* [1]

Moonlight spilled around His supplicating form, framing His earnest, upturned face with its silvery light, illuminating the eyes that were, themselves, "lighted up with unutterable love." [2] Palm and pomegranate trees wept down dew, and the night breezes sighed in sympathy as their Creator, "with strong crying and tears ... prayed for His disciples and"—amazingly—"for Himself." [3] In concert with His cries, the night creatures sang their mournful songs until the rising sun sent them to their dens, and summoned Jesus for another day of punishing spiritual warfare. Having unburdened all of His cares and crushing sorrows in "the secret place of the Most High," He came forth filled with spiritual vigor, braced for whatever the day might bring Him (Psalm 91:1).

Such was the pattern of Jesus' prayer life that He invariably spent hours communing with His Father, and not infrequently spent the entire night in prayer. It is one of the many ironies of His incarnation that He, the Master of moon and sun, Sustainer of all things animate and inanimate, should Himself need to pray for emotional and spiritual sustenance. Yet "as one with us, a sharer in our needs and weaknesses, He was wholly dependent upon God."[4] Having become a brother in our infirmities, "in all points tempted as we are" (Hebrews 4:15), Jesus' "humanity made prayer a necessity and a privilege."[5] But the picture is more comprehensive still: While Jesus prayed for Himself, it was never as an end in itself, but for the sake of those He had come to save. As the Redeemer and representative of humanity, everything Jesus did was in our behalf:

> "In Christ the cry of humanity reached the Father of infinite pity. As a man He supplicated the throne of God till His humanity was charged with a heavenly current that should connect humanity with divinity. Through continual communion He received life from God, that He might impart life to the world. His experience is to be ours."[6]

Jesus' prayer life was the cable that connected humanity with divinity, infusing Him with "a heavenly current" of life that was felt by all with whom He came in contact. As He communed with His beloved Father, He was filled with "the boundless resources of Omnipotence," that He might enrich our spiritually impoverished world with the treasures of salvation. But the startling auxiliary truth is that His extraordinary prayer experience "is to be ours." Both a challenge and a promise, this incredible assertion tells us that God both calls us, and will enable us, to be Christ's intercessory ambassadors of reconciliation in an alienated world. Yet how to experience such prevailing prayer?

The little book *Steps to Christ* tells us that "there are certain conditions upon which we may expect that God will hear and answer our prayers."[7] These "conditions" exist, not because God is unwilling to answer prayer, but because He needs to make us into people who can be entrusted with the boundless resources of His heavenly storehouse. So He patiently teaches us the *principles* of prevailing prayer, that we may understand how to handle this powerful "key in the hand of faith." He teaches us that:

We must feel our need of help from Him. Prayer without a sense of need is a sterile pretense that can't receive God's blessings because it doesn't really *want* them. Augustine said that God is always trying to give us good things, but our hands are too full to receive them. Prayer without a sense of need is a clenched hand in the face of God, too satisfied with its own imagined fullness to open itself to His life-giving grace. But while sin has tricked us into believing that we are "rich" and "have need of nothing" (Revelation 3:17), God is constantly trying to help us see "our great need"—which "is itself an argument" that "pleads most eloquently in our behalf." [8]

If we're cherishing known sin, He can't answer us. Isaiah said to backslidden Israel: "Behold, the Lord's hand is not shortened, that it cannot save; nor His ear heavy, that it cannot hear. But your *iniquities* have separated you from your God; and your *sins* have hidden His face from you, so that He will not hear" (Isaiah 59:1, 2, italics added). For God to answer our prayers while we habitually engage in *known* sin would make Him a participant in our sin, and have the effect of hardening us in rebellion. God is love, and for that very reason He is infinitely motivated to separate us from the sin that destroys us. As C.S. Lewis has observed, "Love is something more stern and splendid than mere kindness," which "cares not whether its object becomes good or bad, provided only that it escapes suffering." [9] While God would love to answer our prayers in a way that spares us from suffering and hardship, He wants even more to cleanse us from the sin that brings so much unnecessary suffering into our lives and into the lives of others.

We are to pray in faith. Paul tells us that "without faith it is impossible to please Him, for he who comes to God must believe that He is, and that He is a rewarder of those who diligently seek Him" (Hebrews 11:6). Why is this so? Because God has made us *rational* beings—if we either don't believe that He exists, or if we believe that He's a "hard man" (Matthew 25:24) who callously refuses to respond to His dependent creatures, we have effectually prevented ourselves from receiving anything good at His hands. "Faith which works by *love*" discerns the gracious character of the One it entreats. Recognizing God's unmerited favor in His gift of life and that which sustains it, faith nourishes itself in the "atmosphere of grace" with which God has encircled our world. As it reposes in that which it has learned to appreciate about God, it risks itself in that which is not yet clear, confident that the benevolent character of God is intrinsically consistent and reliable.

If we cherish an unforgiving spirit in our hearts, God can't answer our prayers. Guilty, every one, of the death of Christ, who "Himself bore *our* sins in His own body on the tree," we are nevertheless objects of the astonishing forgiveness of God, who has not imputed our trespasses against us (1 Peter 2:24, italics added; see 2 Corinthians 5:19). So in imitation of our Lord, we are under sacred obligation to extend that same spirit of forgiveness to others, "however sorely they may have wounded us"—"whether or not they confess their faults."[10] If, like the ungrateful servant (see Matthew 18:22–35), we refuse to forgive our brothers and sisters after God has so graciously forgiven us, we prevent Him from making His forgiveness effective in our lives, because "he who is unforgiving cuts off the very channel through which alone he can receive mercy from God."[11] And if we cut ourselves off from God's mercy, we've obviously severely limited His ability to respond to our prayers.

We are to pray with consistency and perseverance. "If the Saviour of men, with His divine strength, felt the need of prayer, how much more should feeble, sinful mortals feel the necessity of prayer—fervent, constant prayer!" [12] Beset by a sinful nature from within, inundated by alluring temptations from without, and relentlessly dogged by a devil who "walks about like a roaring lion, seeking whom he may devour," we desperately need constant communion with God (1 Peter 5:8). Both our privilege and our necessity, "*unceasing prayer* is the unbroken union of the soul with God, so that life from God flows into our life; and from our life, purity and holiness flow back to God." [13] Such prayer is, in short, "the life of the soul" [14] —and in turn becomes the breath of life to our world.

We are to pray in Jesus' name. To pray in Jesus' name "is to pray in the *mind and spirit* of Jesus, while we believe His promises, rely upon His grace, and work His works." [15] It is to pray, not only in the secret place of private prayer, but as an integrated member of the body of Christ, and as an interceding member "of the great web of humanity"—as "no one prays aright who seeks a blessing for himself alone." [16] Carried on the wings of Christ's righteousness, prayer that is *truly* offered in Jesus' name is the "prayer of a righteous man [that] avails much," as Jesus is that Righteous Man who both inspires and mediates every effective, fervent prayer (James 5:16).

There are times when it is appropriate to fast. "When Christ was the most fiercely beset by temptation, He ate nothing. He committed Himself to God and, through earnest prayer and perfect submission to the will of His Father, came off conqueror." [17] Christ's experience and the biblical record teach us that during times of intense spiritual warfare and deep soul-searching, abstaining from food can help us maintain our spiritual focus. Yet we must be careful not to turn fasting into a kind of penance that we think will earn us points with God. "The spirit of true fasting and prayer is the spirit which yields mind, heart, and will to God." [18] In its more comprehensive sense, fasting is an abstemious, self-denying lifestyle that is fully invested in Christian service, as per the "true fast" of Isaiah 58:

> "Is this not the fast that I have chosen: To loose the bonds of wickedness, to undo the heavy burdens, to let the oppressed go free, and that you break every yoke? Is it not to share your bread with the hungry, and that you bring to your house the poor who are cast out; when you see the naked, that you cover him, and not hide yourself from your own flesh?" (Isaiah 58:6, 7, italics added).

We are to praise and thank God! It comes almost as a shock to us to remember, preoccupied as we become by all of our perplexities and concerns, that we have so much for which to be thankful! Yet we are the subjects of inexhaustible grace, continually mediated to us by a soon-coming Savior with whom we'll spend an eternity of bliss. Life can be heartbreakingly hard; it's true. But God is good, and it's good for us to remember it!

In summary, inspiration and the example of Jesus teach us that the "prevailing prayer" briefly outlined above is the breath of life that oxygenates our own spiritual experience, and helps to generate church-wide revival, which, not surprisingly, "need be expected only in answer to *prayer*"—"not because God is not willing to bestow His blessing upon us, but because we are unprepared to receive it." [19]

While God is more eager than we can imagine to rain righteousness down on this spiritually drought-plagued earth, we are the ones who must learn to appreciate the privilege of being His co-workers. We are the ones who must have our eyes opened to the value of the boundless resources of Omnipotence, that we may wisely employ this singular key in the hand of faith.

Endnotes

1. Ellen G. White, *Steps to Christ*, pp. 94–95.

2. Ellen G. White, *Testimonies to the Church*, Volume 5, p. 253.

3. Ellen G. White, *Testimonies to the Church*, Volume 2, p. 508.

4. Ellen G. White, *The Desire of Ages*, p. 363.

5. *Steps to Christ*, p. 94.

6. *The Desire of Ages*, p. 363.

7. *Steps to Christ*, p. 95.

8. *Ibid.*

9. C.S. Lewis, *The Problem of Pain* (New York: HarperCollins Publishers, 2001), p. 32.

10. Ellen G. White, *Thoughts From the Mount of Blessing*, p. 114.

11. *Ibid.*, p. 113.

12. *Testimonies to the Church*, Volume 2, p. 202.

13. *Steps to Christ*, p. 98.

14. *Ibid.* (italics added).

15. *Ibid.*, p. 101 (italics added).

16. *Thoughts From the Mount of Blessing*, p. 105.

17. *Testimonies to the Church*, Volume 2, p. 202.

18. Ellen G. White, *Counsels on Diet and Foods*, p. 189, (MS 28, 1900).

19. Ellen G. White, *Selected Messages, Book One*, p. 121 (italics added).

Truth and Spirit

Chapter Thirteen
Promises, Promises

> *"His divine power has given to us all things that
> pertain to life and godliness, through the knowledge
> of Him who called us by glory and virtue, by which
> have been given to us exceedingly great and precious
> promises, that through these you may be partakers
> of the divine nature, having escaped the corruption
> that is in the world through lust."*
>
> —2 Peter 1:3, 4

A shout of admiration rang out from the restless throng
as Aaron unveiled his molten masterpiece. Gilded by
the setting Sinai sun, the virile form of a golden bull
rose from its lofty pedestal, its nostrils belligerently flared, its
pugnacious eyes glittering sightlessly, a sun disk cradled between
its sinuously curving horns. [1] Prostrating itself in adoration, the
crowd cried exultantly, "This is your *god*, O Israel, that brought
you out of the land of Egypt!" (Exodus 32:4, italics added).
Flattered that his creation had been so well received, and swept
into the popular frenzy, Aaron went so far as to build an altar
of sacrifice before the graven creature, then triumphantly
proclaimed, "Tomorrow is a feast to the Lord" (Verse 5).

Pulsing with excitement, the Israelites impatiently passed the
night. At sunrise, they streamed from their tents to offer sacrifices
to their depiction of divinity—a merciless, brutish creature

revered for its sexual potency and savage strength. In keeping with their conceptualization of God, their "worship" soon degenerated into a drunken celebration of unfettered sensuality. As far as they were concerned, "revival" had arrived in all its glory and they were but surrendering to the movings of the spirit.

Tucked away in a cleft of Mount Sinai, wrapped in the glorious embrace of the true God, Moses was oblivious to the anarchy that was sweeping the camp. For 40 days he had been locked in communion with the Lord, who had laid out for him the master plan of the sanctuary and its services. Having just engraved onto tables of stone—with His own finger—the 10 timeless precepts He had thundered from Sinai's flaming peak, the Lord tersely informed His mediator, "Go, get down! For your people whom you brought out of the land of Egypt have corrupted themselves. They have turned aside quickly out of the way which I commanded them" (v. 7).

After interceding, Christlike for "his" rebellious people, Moses hurried down the mountain to find them writhing in a pagan frenzy before their glittering god. Righteously indignant, he smashed the sacred tablets before them—a fitting symbol of the covenant they had so "quickly" and callously broken, having three times solemnly promised a few short weeks before: "All that the Lord has said we will do, and be obedient" (Exodus 24:7; see 19:8, 24:3).

What had gone wrong? How had the people's earnest resolve so quickly evaporated into reckless abandon? Ellen White gives us some insight:

> "The people did not realize the sinfulness of their own hearts, and that without Christ it was impossible for them to keep God's law; and they readily entered into covenant with God. Feeling that they were able to establish their own righteousness, they declared, 'All that the Lord hath said will we do, and be obedient.'" [2]

Not realizing the "sinfulness of their own hearts," the Israelites had rashly entered into covenant relation with God, not on the basis of faith in *His* precious promises to them, but on the basis of *their* presumptuous promises to Him. It was an arrangement that was destined to fail. It was, in fact, what the Bible calls the old, or "first," covenant. As Paul has explained in the book of Hebrews: "If there had been nothing wrong with that first covenant, no place would have been sought for another. But God found fault with the people" (Hebrews 8:7, 8 NIV). God found fault with the *people* (as opposed to His law) because they were incapable, of themselves, of honoring the covenant they had naively entered into. As Doug Batchelor has said, "The problem with the Old Covenant was the faulty promises of the people and their inability to keep God's laws through their own strength."[3]

Ellen White concurs:

> "The terms of the 'old covenant' were, Obey and live: 'If a man do, he shall even live in them' (Ezekiel 20:11; Leviticus 18:5); but 'cursed be he that confirmeth not all the words of this law to do them.' Deuteronomy 27:26."[4]

"Revival" that rests on the flimsy foundation of our faithless promises to God, or on an "unwieldy combination of the promise of God *and* the … promises of people,"[5] is destined to be a flash in the pan, whether it flames out in reckless abandon or peters out into Laodicean lukewarm-ness. Either way, such old covenant religion is doomed to dismal failure. As E.J. Waggoner has nailed it:

> "That which makes all the trouble is that even when [people] are willing to recognize the Lord at all they want to make bargains with Him. They want it to be an equal, 'mutual' affair—a

transaction in which they can consider themselves on a par with God. But whoever deals with God must deal with Him on His own terms, that is, on a basis of fact—that we have nothing and are nothing, and He has everything and is everything and gives everything.[6]

Once again, this is our starting point in revival—God has and is everything, we have and are nothing, spiritually and morally speaking. Far from inspiring us to make rash promises of humanistic obedience, a confrontation with Sinai should convince us of our utter moral bankruptcy and innate hostility to God's law, and drive us to our knees in helpless humility. As this happens, we will be prepared to receive God's glorious gospel solution—the *new* covenant, which is a "*better* covenant" because it is "established on *better* promises," even the promises of God (Hebrews 8:6, italics added):

> "The 'new covenant' was established upon 'better promises'—the promise of forgiveness of sins and of the grace of God to renew the heart and bring it into harmony with the principles of God's law. "This shall be the covenant that *I* will make with the house of Israel; After those days, saith the Lord, I will put my law in their inward parts, and write it in their hearts … I will forgive their iniquity, and will remember their sin no more" (Jeremiah 31:33, 34).[7]

Precious promises! *God's* covenant, which rests on *His* "exceedingly great and precious promises," brings the complete, twofold blessing of forgiveness for sin *and* a heart reconciled to the principles of His law. His promises form the sure foundation of the only true covenant—the "everlasting covenant" that the Godhead established at "the foundation of the world," unveiled at the inception of sin, and has faithfully maintained throughout history (Revelation 13:8). All of humanity's attempts to "improve" upon this arrangement have been mere humanistic detours away from God's promise-powered "covenant of grace," [8] the only one that works.

When we, by faith, enter into this everlasting covenant of grace, *all* of God's commands become promises, all His biddings become enablings. That which was written on tables of stone is now engraved on the tender tablets of the heart, which has been softened by the subduing grace of Christ. The externalized law that could only condemn us as transgressors, now becomes the living, internalized character of God, such that we say with the psalmist, "I *delight* to do Your will, O my God, and Your law is *within my heart*" (Psalm 40:8, italics added).

When the principles of God's law are received in this proper context of "grace … through faith," they become the catalyst for authentic, lasting revival and thorough reformation (Ephesians 2:8). They are the means by which we become "partakers of the divine nature," and are enabled to escape "the corruption that is in the world through lust" (2 Peter 1:4). They are the means by which we become recipients of the very "mind" of Christ, as we'll discuss in our next chapter.

Endnotes

1. "The word translated 'calf' in the [Exodus 32] narrative refers more specifically to a young bull. Thus the choice may well have related to the practice of bull worship, which was prevalent in ancient Egypt and Canaan. Fearsomely strong, notoriously quick-tempered, bulls were revered throughout much of the ancient world as symbols of strength and fertility. The bull appears in the art and sacred texts of Syria, Mesopotamia, and Egypt." http://www.bible-history.com/tabernacle/TAB4untitled00000088.htm

2. Ellen G. White, *Patriarchs and Prophets*, pp. 371–372.

3. Doug Batchelor, *Advindication* (Roseville, CA: Amazing Facts, Inc., 2004), p. 18 (italics in original).

4. *Patriarchs and Prophets*, p. 372.

5. *Advindication*, p. 17.

6. E.J. Waggoner, *The Glad Tidings* (Mountain View, CA: Pacific Press Publishing Association, 1978) p. 71.

7. *Patriarchs and Prophets*, p. 372 (italics added).

8. *Ibid.*, p. 370.

Chapter Fourteen
Let This Mind Be in You

"Do not be conformed to this world, but be transformed by the renewing of your mind, that you may prove what is that good and acceptable and perfect will of God."

—Romans 12:2

"The average human brain weighs about three-and-a-half pounds. It's roughly the size of a large head of cauliflower, and resembles, in color and consistency, a generous blob of extra-firm tofu." [1] A mass of convoluted folds, fissures, and bulges, its two fleshy hemispheres married by a tough, fibrous band called the corpus callosum, the whole spongy package is cushioned by a thin layer of fluid and anchored by ligaments to the bony skull. Unglamorous, perhaps; yet blobby, bulgy, unglamorous appearance notwithstanding, the brain is certainly the most fascinating, elegant organ of the body.

Amazing enough that this unlikely little powerhouse almost effortlessly orchestrates our every voluntary and involuntary physiological function. Yet more amazing still, this tangible, physical organ straddles the threshold between the seen and the unseen by translating our encounters with the material world into intangible thoughts, feelings, and memories. Almost miraculously, "the structures of the brain operate harmoniously to turn raw sensory data into an integrated perception of the world outside the skull: the *brain* is a collection of physical structures that gather and process sensory, cognitive, and emotional data; the *mind* is the phenomenon of thoughts, memories, and emotions that arise from the perceptual processes of the brain."[2]

In short, "Brain makes mind. ... Without the brain's ability to process various types of input in highly sophisticated ways, the thoughts and feelings that constitute the mind would simply not exist."[3] What are the implications of this brain-mind relationship with regard to our spiritual life? Just this: "There's no other way for God to get into your head except through the brain's neural pathways."[4] Through the physical organ of the *brain*, "the citadel of the being,"[5] God communicates with our *minds*, and so makes Himself and His ways known to us. Our spirituality is experienced in the same way that we experience all of life—in the context of our neurophysiologic set-up.

So how does God use our brain's neural pathways to "get into our heads"? While He is infinitely flexible and inventive when it comes to getting our attention, His primary modus operandi is to inculcate our minds with the principles of His Word, as facilitated by His Holy Spirit (who we'll talk more about in the next chapter). The "exceedingly great and precious promises" that we discussed in our last chapter carry within them the very *principles of life* that are able to make us partakers of His divine nature. These life-giving principles saturate and illuminate His *Word*, from beginning to end. As we prayerfully and thoughtfully study this Word, our minds are strengthened, elevated, invigorated and ennobled. In short, they are *transformed*:

> There is nothing more calculated to strengthen the intellect than the study of the Scriptures. No other book is so potent to elevate the thoughts, to give vigor to the faculties, as the broad, ennobling

truths of the Bible. If God's word were studied as
it should be, men would have a breadth of mind,
a nobility of character, and a stability of purpose
rarely seen in these times.[6]

All of this is possible because God's "power, *His very life,*
dwells in His word."[7] Yet this is true of God's Word, not simply
because it's full of life-giving principles, but because these
principles proceed from and describe the person of *Jesus,* the
living, breathing Word. As He told the Bible students of His
day, "You search the Scriptures, for in them you think you have
eternal life; and *these are they which testify of Me*" (John 5:39, italics
added). The Bible is the premier source of mind-transforming
eternal life, because it is a Book about Jesus, the Source of life,
and as we appreciatively behold Him in it, we become changed
into His likeness.

> Let the mind dwell upon [Christ's] love, upon the
> beauty, the perfection, of His character. Christ
> in His self-denial, Christ in His humiliation,
> Christ in His purity and holiness, Christ in His
> matchless love—this is the subject for the soul's
> contemplation. It is by loving Him, copying Him,
> depending wholly upon Him, that you are to be
> transformed into His likeness.[8]

This is the process through which we receive the "mind of
Christ." As we *behold* Him in His Word and consent to have
our hearts drawn out in appreciation, beholding becomes
identification, and identification becomes *emulation.*[9] As
emulation becomes habitual, actions continually reinforce
thinking, which urges us on to further action—which amounts
to the formation of *character,* because in the final analysis, "it is
through *action* that character is built."[10]

In other words, not only does brain make mind, but mind makes brain, as the thoughts and feelings it generates affect brain chemistry and functioning, by stimulating the release of hormones and neurotransmitters, and instigating the formation of new neural pathways. [11] More than this, mind ultimately makes the *whole person*, as the behaviors we choose to engage in affect our entire physiological make-up and determine the probability of future behavior. Solomon aptly captured this dynamic psycho-physiological reciprocity when he said, "As he thinks in his heart, so *is* he" (Proverbs 23:7).[12] As we think, so we do; as we do, so we become; and as we become, so we think. Such is the cycle of character formation, and it carries immense personal and social implications, for now and for eternity.

While all of that is the basic "how" of receiving the mind, or character, of Christ, let's discuss now about the "what"—*what* sort of mind is the mind of Christ? What are its distinguishing characteristics?

It's a mind that is agape driven. Paul said to the Philippians, "Let this *mind* be in you which was also in Christ Jesus, who ... made Himself of no reputation, taking the form of a bondservant;" He "humbled Himself and became obedient to the point of death, even the death of the cross" (Philippians 2:5, 7, 8, italics added). The mind of Christ is a mind that is *monolithically* motivated by *agape*, which, as we discussed in chapter 4, is a heaven-born love that gives itself away to the uttermost, that it might bless the other at its own expense. To be indwelt by the mind of Christ is to continually, intentionally *choose* love, whatever the cost to ourselves, until it becomes our second nature. "When self is merged in Christ, love springs forth spontaneously. The completeness of Christian character is attained when the impulse to help and bless others springs constantly from within." [13]

It's a mind that comprehends the whole, paradoxical nature of truth. Sin has had the effect of fracturing our ability to comprehend the internal unity of truth. As we are reconciled to God, we are also restored to our "right minds"—the mind that humanity had before sin brought alienation and fragmentation. Christ had this reconciled mind, a mind in which law and grace, faith and works, and every other apparent Bible contradiction was comprehended in its paradoxical wholeness. Having fully entrusted Himself to His Father, He was free of the pride and insecurity that compels us to defensively adhere to one pole of truth at the expense of the other. As we likewise entrust ourselves to Christ, who "Himself embodies and exhibits truth's paradoxical nature," [14] we will be reconciled to truth in its paradoxical fullness, and in the process, be reconciled to each other.

It's a mind that overcomes sin, even in sinful flesh. Jesus grappled with sin in the context of our sin-impacted neurophysiologic framework. Having subjugated His divinity to the limitations of fallen humanity, He interacted with God through the same "neural pathways" that we must, and experienced character development as we all do, by continually "bringing every thought into captivity" to the Word and will of God (2 Corinthians 10:5).

As A.T. Jones has summarized it:

> Where the victory comes, where the battle-field is, is right upon the line between the flesh and the mind. The battle is fought in the realm of the *thoughts.* ... Therefore Jesus Christ came in just such flesh as ours, but with a mind that held its integrity against every temptation, against every inducement to sin—a mind that never consented to sin—no, never in the least conceivable shadow

of a thought. And by that means he has brought that divine mind to every [person] on earth. Therefore every [person] for the choosing and by the choosing, can have that divine mind that conquers sin in the flesh. [15]

What a privilege—that God would condescend to share His *mind* with undeserving rebels such as us! And what a miracle—that He can, indeed, so transform minds fractured and depraved by sin that we can be brought back into loving, obedient fellowship with Him! While the implications of the process of character development are very sobering indeed, we can be encouraged that God is even more motivated than we are to see His image recreated in us. And we can be assured that He's constantly working to bring it about through the most powerful regenerating Agent in the universe—His Holy Spirit.

Endnotes

1. Andrew Newberg, M.D., Eugene D'Aquili, M.D., PhD., and Vince Rause, *Why God Won't Go Away: Brain Science and the Biology of Belief* (New York: Ballantine Books, 2001), p. 17.

2. *Ibid.*, p. 33 (italics in original).

3. *Ibid.*

4. *Why God Won't Go Away*, p. 37. Of course, the devil uses these same neural pathways to "get into our heads," which is why must be very selective about what we make the focus of our attention.

5. Ellen G. White, *Counsels to Parents, Teachers, and Students*, p. 299.

6. Ellen G. White, *Steps to Christ*, p. 90.

7. Ellen G. White, *Thoughts From the Mount of Blessing*, p. 150 (italics added).

8. *Steps to Christ*, p. 70.

9. This process is basically what psychology calls observational learning, with a strong cognitive component; it is also what the Bible refers to, in so many words, as the process of discipling.

10. *Thoughts From the Mount of Blessing*, p. 149 (italics added). Interestingly, the word "character" in "We also glory in tribulations, knowing that tribulation produces

perseverance; and perseverance, character; and character, hope" (Romans 5:3, 4), is translated from the Greek *dokime*, which basically means "experience."

11. Recent studies using PET scans have demonstrated that patients treated for major depression with appropriate psychotherapy experienced changes in brain functioning similar to those experienced by depressed patients treated with antidepressant medication, indicating that the mere act of *thinking* carries neurochemical and physiological implications. See Don H. and Sandra E. Hockenbury, *Psychology* (New York: Worth Publishers, 2003), p. 656.

12. The word "heart" in this verse is translated from the Hebrew *nephesh*, which is commonly used in the Old Testament for "soul" (meaning the whole being), and sometimes for "mind."

13. Ellen G. White, *Christ's Object Lessons*, p. 384.

14. A. Leroy Moore, *Adventism in Conflict*, (Hagerstown, MD: Review and Herald Publishing Association, 1995) p. 43. Thanks to Dr. Moore, who has patiently labored to help me understand the paradoxical nature of truth.

15. A.T. Jones, *General Conference Bulletin*, 1895, pp. 328–329 (italics added).

Chapter Fifteen
Born of the Spirit

"That which is born of the flesh is flesh, and that which is born of the Spirit is spirit. Do not marvel that I said to you, 'You must be born again.'"

—John 3:6, 7

Gathering the flowing folds of his cloak tightly about him, the old Pharisee slipped into the moonless night. Silently he crept through the narrow, twisted streets of the Upper City, dodging an amber pool of lantern light, tiptoeing past an unshuttered window. Through a North Wall gate he glided like a specter, until he caught his foot on a rough step and barely stifled a cry of pain. Limping now, he felt, more than saw, his way along the blackness of the Temple wall, eluded detection at the Antonia Fortress, and fled past the Pool of Bethesda. Trembling with relief, he crossed the Kidron Valley and clambered up the western slope of the Mount of Olives, to find the Object of his clandestine visit waiting expectantly, as though He Himself had made the appointment.

So Nicodemus, Pharisee of Pharisees, found himself face to face with Jesus. While he dared not approach the controversial young teacher in broad daylight for fear of being made the brunt of his contemporaries' derision, the influential leader nevertheless felt drawn to Jesus, in whose humble presence he now felt surprisingly intimidated. Composing himself, he cleared his throat and began his interview with a cautious affirmation, "Rabbi, we know that You are a teacher come from God; for no one can do these signs that You do unless God is with him."

Detecting the fragile sense of conviction beneath the careful dignity, Jesus sent His first arrow flying straight to the mark: "Most assuredly, I say to you, unless one is born again, he cannot see the kingdom of God."

Nicodemus was affronted. Not only was he a member in good standing of the august and powerful Sanhedrin, he was a sincerely moral man who hadn't risked his reputation to be lectured about his "spirituality" by a young upstart. Annoyed at Jesus' boldness, the old ruler attempted to deflect this blow to his pharisaical pride by sarcastically replying, "'How can a man be born when he is old? Can he enter a second time into his mother's womb and be born?'"

Declining the bait, Jesus drove home His point with greater emphasis, "Most assuredly, I say to you, unless one is born of water and the Spirit, he cannot enter the kingdom of God. That which is born of the flesh is flesh, and that which is born of the Spirit is spirit. Do not marvel that I said to you, " 'You must be born again.'" The wind blows where it wishes, and you hear the sound of it, but cannot tell where it comes from and where it goes. So is everyone who is born of the Spirit."

Like the Spirit they described, the Savior's enigmatic words rushed into Nicodemus' startled mind like a fresh, sharp breeze, disarming his pride, subduing his heart, until, in spite of himself, the Pharisee wondered aloud, "How can these things be?"

To His now-receptive audience of one, Jesus delivered His immortal synopsis of salvation: "As Moses lifted up the serpent in the wilderness, even so must the Son of Man be lifted up, that whoever believes in Him should not perish but have eternal life. For God so loved the world that He gave His only begotten Son, that whoever believes in Him should not perish but have everlasting life."[1]

It was a spiritual watershed for Nicodemus, who strode back through the darkened streets of Jerusalem with the living seed of truth planted deep within his wondering soul. Silently it took root in the years following, as he pondered the significance of Jesus' words and quietly observed His ministry. And when at last he witnessed the saving sight of Jesus being sacrificially "lifted up" on Calvary's cross for *his* sins, that small seed budded and burst into bloom, and the cautious Pharisee became a bold, devoted disciple.

Yet what made it all happen? What sort of force could be so fierce and yet so gentle that it could both compel and win such a hesitating heart? Not surprisingly, the Agent of Nicodemus' regeneration was none other than the mysterious Holy Spirit to whom Jesus had introduced him that moonless midnight, amidst the restlessly swaying olive branches and the sweetly sighing summer breeze. It was the Spirit of God who, invisibly and unobtrusively, conveyed Jesus' words into his doubting mind, all the while illuminating and reassuring, convicting and convincing. It was the Holy Spirit who inspired Nicodemus' fragile faith, and nurtured it in the secret places of his soul. And it was the same Spirit who, acting as divine midwife, delivered this brand-new babe in Christ when the catalyst of the cross awakened his consent to be "born again."

So it is with all who consent to the process:

> "By an agency as unseen as the wind, Christ is constantly working upon the heart. Little by little, perhaps unconsciously to the receiver, impressions are made that tend to draw the soul to Christ. These may be received through meditating upon Him, through reading the Scriptures, or through hearing the word from the living preacher. Suddenly, as the Spirit comes with more direct appeal, the soul gladly surrenders itself to Jesus. By many this is called sudden conversion; but it is

the result of long wooing by the Spirit of God—a patient, protracted process."[2]

The divine Lover of our souls is "constantly" and tirelessly at work, bringing His truth and love to bear on fallen humanity, striving to awaken us from our sin-induced death and decline. He is the One who brings revival, who breathes eternal life into our otherwise ephemeral existence, who births us into joyful union with God. Far from being some sterile transaction in a heavenly ledger book, the new birth is a real and radical *experience* of personal transformation:

> "Like the wind, which is invisible, yet the effects of which are plainly seen and felt, is the Spirit of God in its work upon the human heart. That regenerating power, which no human eye can see, begets a *new life* in the soul; it creates a *new being* in the image of God. While the work of the Spirit is silent and imperceptible, its effects are manifest. If the heart has been renewed by the Spirit of God, the life will bear witness to the fact."[3]

Perhaps it would be well to pause and recall that when humanity expelled God's indwelling Spirit, we became subject to two very serious consequences: We developed an intrinsic hatred of God's authority over our lives, and we became deceived into distrusting His benevolent character. Ever after, we've found ourselves caught in a vicious, self-perpetuating cycle of enmity, deception, and alienation from which we can never independently extricate ourselves. Our only solution is to allow the Holy Spirit to reenter our lives and compensate for our deficiencies, by both subduing our natural enmity and enlightening us with the truth about God's character.

So He "begets new life in the soul" by indwelling it with His own reconciling, enlightening presence. He overcomes our natural, or carnal, mind with His spiritual mind—even the mind of Christ. While "the carnal mind is enmity against God; for it is not subject to the law of God, nor indeed can be," the "mind of the Spirit" brings us into harmony with God, "that the righteous requirement of the law might be fulfilled in us who do not walk according to the flesh but according to the Spirit" (Romans 8:7, 27, 4).

It is the Holy Spirit's winsome, wooing presence that turns the promises of God and the principles of His Word into effective instruments of transformation. Through the skillful facilitation of "the only effectual teacher of divine truth,"[4] the letter of the law is married to the spirit, and we become the blessed recipients of an integrated package of vibrant, transforming truth. When this happens, we won't be able to *keep* our transformed minds from expressing themselves through our behavior. Our lives will "bear witness to the fact" that we have been with Jesus.

Though it might take time for some deeply entrenched habits and thought processes to be corrected, there will be a continual, intentional turning away from known sin, because the Spirit of Christ is a sin-overcoming Spirit. The Author of our faith is also its Finisher: He would never rescue us from the penalty of sin only to leave us in the grip of its power. So while we may at times take two steps back for every three steps forward, God has assured us that as we consistently behold "the glory [or character] of the Lord," we will indeed be "transformed into the same image from glory to glory, just as by the Spirit of the Lord" (2 Corinthians 3:18).

Endnotes

1. Dialogue taken from John 3:2–9, 14–16; see 3:1–21 for the whole story.

2. Ellen G. White, *The Desire of Ages*, p. 172.

3. Ellen G. White, *Steps to Christ*, p. 57 (italics supplied).

4. *Ibid.*, p. 91.

Chapter Sixteen
One Accord

"I do not pray for these alone, but also for those who will believe in Me through their word; that they all may be one, as You, Father, are in Me, and I in You; that they also may be one in Us, that the world may believe that You sent Me."

—John 17:20, 21

While the regenerating presence of the Holy Spirit in an individual life always results in personal transformation, what are the implications of a *corporate* encounter with God's transforming Spirit? In a word—*Pentecost*. The dramatic revivals experienced by the infant church after Christ's ascension were the product of a corporate infilling of the Holy Spirit that repeatedly rebirthed and multiplied itself. Yet something crucial preceded and, in fact, made possible this corporate infilling. And that was a precious and seldom seen commodity known as *unity*.

Something happened between Passover and Pentecost, between the cross and the coming of the Comforter—something that transformed the 11 remaining disciples from a loosely knit aggregate of competitive, self-serving egotists into a tightly knit team of cooperative, self-sacrificing servants. Something wonderfully unprecedented happened, such that it could be said of them, "No longer were they a collection of independent units or discordant, conflicting elements. No longer were their hopes set on worldly greatness. They were *of 'one accord,' 'of one heart and of one soul.'* "[1]

We can't help but wonder, What sort of miracle would enable 11 small, autonomous hearts to become so synchronized that they could beat as one great heart to the glory of God?

The book *The Acts of the Apostles* gives us some insight into the disciples' experience following Christ's departing command to "Tarry in the city of Jerusalem until you are endued with power from on high" (Luke 24:49). Ecstatically happy that their beloved Lord was not only *alive*, but about to empower them to evangelize the world, the 11 and their 120 fellow believers jubilantly returned to the Upper Room—not to barricade themselves inside "for fear of the Jews," as they had done previously, but to actively cooperate with God by letting Him make them into the kind of people who could be entrusted with world-changing power. This they did by engaging in a process of soul-searching and faith-stretching that followed a basic pattern: [2]

1. **They were "continually in the temple praising and blessing God" (Luke 24:53).** While all of Jerusalem expected the disciples to behave like a defeated, dispirited band of mourners, as they had done after Christ's crucifixion, they were shocked to see them celebrating like victors. But the disciples knew something that the rest of Jerusalem didn't. "They knew that they had a Representative in heaven, an Advocate at the throne of God;" so "higher and still higher they extended the hand of faith," [3] praising God that they were "blessed … with every spiritual blessing in the heavenly places in Christ" (Ephesians 1:3). Though they had not yet received visible evidence of the promised blessing, they knew that they surely would, because where Christ resided, *there* was "the substance of things hoped for, the evidence of things not seen" (Hebrews 11:1).

2. ***They meditated on Christ's life and made it the subject of their conversation.*** "Who has the heart? With whom are our thoughts? Of whom do we love to converse? Who has our warmest affections and our best energies? If we are Christ's, our thoughts are with Him, and our sweetest thoughts are of Him."[4] The more they contemplated and conversed about Christ, the more they identified with Him, the more they wanted to become like Him and share Him with the world. Such is the built-in motivational and transforming power of beholding the One who is "altogether lovely," as the Holy Spirit facilitates and injects life into the process (Song of Solomon 5:16).

3. ***They humbled their hearts in repentance and confessed their unbelief.*** As they considered Christ's compassionate, persevering love toward them, they saw their selfishness and unbelief by contrast. They remembered the many times they had resisted His love, the many times their hard hearts and dull minds had frustrated His best efforts, had pained His sensitive nature and clouded His benevolent face with sadness. They experienced to their core what we so often trumpet, yet fail to grasp—that Christianity is essentially a *relational* religion, in which our attitudes and behaviors impact the heart and mind of a living God who has fully invested Himself in reclaiming us for fellowship with Him. Against the backdrop of Jesus' intensely personal and palpable *agape*, they abhorred their immaturity and self-absorption, and experienced a vital, godly repentance that "was not to be repented of" (2 Corinthians 7:10).

4. ***They felt that no sacrifice for their Lord would be too great, and determined to confess Him to the world.*** While we can never undo or atone for the past, we can, by God's grace, allow Him to *redeem* it through us. So the disciples determined that, while they couldn't change what had

come before, they would let it catalyze them to do better. Resolutely turning from "those things which are behind and reaching forward to those things which are ahead," they pressed "toward the goal for the prize of the upward call of God in Christ Jesus" (Philippians 3:13, 14). What was this goal? To bring the saving truth of their beloved Master to other sinful, sorrowing souls who were otherwise without hope in a fallen world.

5. **They prayed together for skill and wisdom to be successful soul-winners.** Realizing that evangelistic success requires relational skill, as well as sincerity and Bible knowledge, the disciples "prayed with intense earnestness for a fitness to meet men [and women] and in their daily intercourse to speak words that would lead sinners to Christ."[5] As they considered the great variety of people and circumstances they would encounter, they recognized that:

> "God's [workers] must be many-sided men [and women]; that is, they must have breadth of character. They are not to be one-idea men [and women], stereotyped in their manner of working, unable to see that their advocacy of truth must vary with the class of people among whom they work and the circumstances they have to meet.[6]

So they prayed for the wisdom, tact, and flexibility to 'become all things to all [people], that [they] might by all means save some' (1 Corinthians 9:22)."

6. *Realizing that such a fitness required that they put "away all differences, all desire for the supremacy," they did just that and "came close in Christian fellowship."*[7] A profession of Christ is nothing but empty posturing if its professors can't even manage to get along with each other. The disciples

recognized that their profession and their witness would be real and credible only if it were lived out to its logical conclusion of Christian unity:

> "Unity existing among the followers of Christ is an *evidence* that the Father has sent His Son to save sinners. It is a *witness* to His power; for nothing short of the miraculous power of God can bring human beings with their different temperaments together in harmonious action, their one aim being to speak the truth in love." [8]

So these individuals with their vastly different temperaments united in their overarching aim to "speak the truth in love." Compelled to rightly represent Christ to each other and to the world, they honestly yet tactfully worked out their differences, for Christ's sake risking vulnerability as they became "as transparent as the sunlight." [9] Their unity was real and substantive because it was not founded on the shifting sand of compromise, but on the firm foundation of true reconciliation, in which the sinful source of estrangement was not just politely tolerated, but thoroughly repented of and dealt with.

The book of Acts joyfully tells us the miraculous outcome of this process of corporate consecration:

> "When the Day of Pentecost had fully come, they were all with one accord in one place. And suddenly there came a sound from heaven, as of a rushing mighty wind, and it filled the whole house where they were sitting. Then there appeared to them divided tongues, as of fire, and one sat upon each of them. And they were all filled with the Holy Spirit and began to speak with other tongues, as the Spirit gave them utterance (Acts 2:1–4).

The Apostles and their 120 brothers and sisters in Christ eagerly "grasped the imparted gift. And what followed? The sword of the Spirit, newly edged with power and bathed in the lightnings of heaven, cut its way through unbelief. *Thousands were converted in a day.*" [10] Not only that, but *practical* demonstrations of Christianity were seen on every hand, as "all who believed … had all things in common, and sold their possessions and goods, and divided them among all, as anyone had need" (Acts 2:44, 45). The unity, benevolence, and spirituality of the Christians became legend, as they "continued daily *with one accord* in the temple," together "ate their food with gladness and simplicity of heart," and by the power of God performed "many wonders and signs" and "added to the church daily those who were being saved" (Acts 2:46, 43, 47, italics added).

Is it any wonder that Ellen White has exclaimed, "What tremendous consequences to the world depend upon the unity of those who claim to be Christians, who claim to believe that the Bible is the Word of God."[11] We can only echo her conviction, and embrace this admonition:

> "Let everyone seek to answer the prayer of Christist:
> 'That they all may be one; as Thou, Father, art in
> Me, and I in Thee.' Oh, what unity is this! and
> says Christ: 'By this shall all men know that ye are
> My disciples, if ye have love one to another.' "[12]

If the dramatic "former rain" revivals of Pentecost sprang up in consequence of the Spirit-led unity of such a small band of believers, what sort of "latter rain" revivals can we expect to experience if we, as a worldwide movement, humbly unite in Christ? While "eye has not seen, nor ear heard" (1 Corinthians 2:9), we can enthusiastically imagine the prospect! Let's resolve then, by His grace, to answer Christ's high priestly prayer for our *corporate* consecration, that we may accurately portray Him to a watching world and facilitate His joyous, soon return.

Endnotes

1. Ellen G. White, *The Acts of the Apostles*, p. 45.

2. As drawn from the chapter "Pentecost" in *The Acts of the Apostles*.

3. *The Acts of the Apostles*, pp. 35, 36.

4. Ellen G. White, *Steps to Christ*, p. 58.

5. *The Acts of the Apostles*, p. 37.

6. Ellen G. White, *Gospel Workers*, p. 119.

7. *The Acts of the Apostles*, p. 37.

8. Ellen G. White, *Testimonies to the Church*, Volume 9, p. 194 (italics added).

9. Ellen G. White, *Thoughts From the Mount of Blessing*, p. 68.

10. *The Acts of the Apostles*, p. 38 (italics added).

11. Ellen G. White, *Sons and Daughters of God*, p. 295.

12. *Testimonies to the Church*, Volume 9, pp. 488–489.

Sharing the Message of Revival

Chapter Seventeen
Christ's Method Alone

> *"Christ's method alone will give true success in reaching the people. The Saviour mingled with men as one who desired their good. He showed His sympathy for them, ministered to their needs, and won their confidence. Then He bade them, 'Follow me.'"*
>
> —Ellen G. White, *The Ministry of Healing*[1]

Cautiously cracking open her door, she darted furtive glances down the deserted village street—more from habit than necessity, as she knew the other women had hours ago made their chatty pilgrimage to the well to get their day's water. Satisfied that she was alone, she hefted her stone water jar to her shoulder and stepped outside, only to be assaulted by the smothering, almost combustible noonday heat. As she padded the half mile to the well, her skin exploded into pinpricks of sweat that quickly turned into rivulets, her nose stung with the pungent, baking scent of dirt and desert scrub; she felt as though she were baking along with them in one vast, sweltering solar oven. It was hard to bear, but easier than bearing the ridicule of the women who apparently felt it their duty to remind her of what she was so acutely aware—that she was an outcast, a pariah, a social leper. Yes, it was easier to bear the heat than their withering company.

But now what was this? A man—and a Jewish man at that—sitting, in this furnace heat, at a Samaritan well! Had she managed to evade the scorn of her countrywomen only to be despised by an arrogant Jewish man? She determined to ignore his very existence, as she went about the business of lowering the pail into the well's cool, limestone recesses and drawing it back up to fill her water pot.

Mission accomplished, she turned on her heel to go, when, incredibly, he asked, "Will you give me a drink?"[2]

She was dumbfounded, yet not quite rendered speechless. Accustomed to speaking her mind to men, she narrowed her eyes suspiciously and answered his question with another, "How is it that You, being a Jew, ask a drink from me, a Samaritan woman?"

Her bold and curious response was just what the man had hoped for. Jesus, for so the Man was, had in fact been studying her intently to determine the key that would unlock her alienated heart.[3] "With the tact born of divine love, He asked, not offered, a favor,"[4] risking rejection in the hope of awakening her trust. Having piqued her interest, He tantalized her with His enigmatic response, "If you knew the gift of God, and who it is who says to you, 'Give Me a drink,' you would have asked Him, and He would have given you living water."

The idea of "living water" was not unfamiliar to the woman. It bespoke of the cool, refreshing streams that bubbled from the few and welcome springs that dotted her arid land. This was language and imagery she could understand, that spoke directly to her felt need, yet that somehow penetrated past it to some inarticulate longing that simmered beneath the surface. Still, as she scrutinized Jesus, she saw only another parched and dusty peasant, who seemed ill-equipped to satisfy His own thirst, let alone hers.

"Sir," she said incredulously, "You have nothing to draw with and the well is deep. Where can you get this living water?" Then she added, as ethnic and sectarian pride asserted itself, "Are You greater than our father Jacob, who gave us the well, and drank from it himself, as well as his sons and his livestock?"

To focus her attention on her emerging sense of need, Jesus repeated and amplified His gospel offer, again couching it in language that was "in harmony with [her] own thought patterns:" [5] "Whoever drinks of this water will thirst again, but whoever drinks of the water that I shall give him will never thirst. But the water that I shall give him will become in him a fountain of water springing up into everlasting life."

It was an incredible assertion, yet it succeeded in fully dredging to the surface her dormant desire for something other, something better than the meager, contentious life to which she'd become accustomed. It painted a vibrant vision into which she couldn't help but project all the fondest, frustrated, most passionate longings of her soul. She didn't understand how He could bring it about, but she knew that she desperately wanted and needed the satisfying, meaningful "everlasting life" this Man had to offer.

"Sir," she pled earnestly, "Give me this water, that I may not thirst, nor come here to draw."

Then Jesus did something that, from a worldly perspective, was inexplicable. With His prospect firmly in the palm of His hand, He declined to clinch the sale, but "abruptly turned the conversation. Before this soul could receive the gift He longed to bestow, she must be brought to recognize her sin and her Saviour." [6]

"Go, call your husband," He solemnly instructed, "and come back."

A tremor of shame passed across her features. "I have no husband," she quietly replied, self-consciously fingering her water pot and averting her eyes from His steady gaze.

"You are right when you say you have no husband," Jesus commended her honesty. "The fact is, you have had five husbands, and the man you now have is not your husband. What you have just said is quite true."

At this, the woman was shaken to her core. She felt a "mysterious hand ... turning the pages of her life history, bringing to view that which she had hoped to keep forever hidden. ... There came to her thoughts of eternity, of the future Judgment, when all that is now hidden shall be revealed. In its light, conscience was awakened."[7] It was a painful, but critical wake-up call: Before she could feel her need of Calvary, she must endure the scrutiny of Sinai, where "all things are naked and open to the eyes of Him to whom we must give account" (Hebrews 4:13).

Reverently she acknowledged, "Sir, I perceive that You are a prophet." Then, hoping to anesthetize the excruciating pangs of conviction, she engaged in the oldest evasion tactic in the book—"she turned to points of religious controversy."[8] Glancing at the ancient ruins of the Samaritan temple on the crest of Mount Gerizim, she assumed an adversarial attitude. "Our fathers worshiped on this mountain, but you Jews claim that the place where we must worship is in Jerusalem."

"Patiently Jesus permitted her to lead the conversation ... meanwhile He watched for the opportunity of again bringing the truth home to her heart."[9] When He sensed an opening, He again anchored the conversation in timeless truth. "Believe me," He said earnestly, "a time is coming when you will worship the Father neither on this mountain nor in Jerusalem. You Samaritans worship what you do not know; we worship what we do know, for salvation is from the Jews."

Far from being an exclusivistic expression of triumphalism, Jesus was making a statement of fact—while the Jews had not, for the most part, incarnated the sacred principles with which they'd been entrusted, nevertheless they were God's repositories of saving truth. The religion of the Samaritans was a confused syncretism of paganism and pure truth that could never accurately represent the character of God, so could never thoroughly lead anyone to Him. If the woman truly wanted to experience the quality of "everlasting life" she so desired, she would have to leave behind even her fondest misconceptions and allow herself to be transformed by both the Spirit and the letter of truth, as Jesus further explained: "Yet a time is coming and has now come when the true worshipers will worship the Father in spirit and truth, for they are the kind of worshipers the Father seeks. God is spirit, and his worshipers must worship in spirit and in truth."

It was enough. She had no more heart to resist. The veil of pride, prejudice, and self-protection was falling away from her consciousness; the conviction of her desperate sinfulness merged with a conviction of Christ's saving graciousness, and she dared to hope that He might be the long-awaited desire of her heart. "I know that Messiah is coming," she said with quiet intensity; "When He comes, He will tell us all things."

Jesus replied simply, "I who speak to you am He."

Wonderingly, the woman gazed at her Messiah, at the clear eyes so radiant with love, at the holy smile that played around the edges of His lips, and she savored the realization—this was her God! Then she exploded into breathless excitement—this news was too good to keep to herself! Abandoning her water jar, she flew back through the furnace heat to put her village on notice. And notwithstanding her outcast status, her transformation spoke such volumes that her neighbors followed this gospel pied piper to the source of the living water that had so satisfied her thirst. At the conclusion of a spontaneous, two-day revival, "many" accepted the offer of living water, both because of the woman's winsome witness and because of Jesus' own witness of Himself.

So the cycle of soul-winning was completed and repeated, many times over, as the newly converted immediately assisted in the conversion of those within her sphere of influence. The woman of Sychar is a shining example to us of the dynamic truth that, "No sooner does one come to Christ than there is born in his heart a desire to make known to others what a precious friend he has found in Jesus; the saving and sanctifying truth cannot be shut up in his heart. If we are clothed with the righteousness of Christ and are filled with the joy of His indwelling Spirit, we shall not be able to hold our peace."[10]

While the woman at the well is a model of motivated soul-winning, Jesus is the model Soul-Winner. His unswerving, incorruptible devotion to truth, combined with His intense concern for the individual object of His evangelistic attention, is the template from which we're to derive our understanding and experience. We can't improve upon the Master's method, which "alone will give true success in reaching the people. The Saviour mingled with men as one who desired their good. He showed His sympathy for them, ministered to their needs, and won their confidence. Then He bade them, 'Follow me.' "[11]

Endnotes

1. Ellen G. White, *The Ministry of Healing*, p. 143.

2. Dialogue taken from John 4:7–26 (italics supplied); some verses taken from the NIV for the sake of readability.

3. "The process of winning the woman of Samaria deserves the most careful study on the part of all who set out to win others to Christ. There were four main stages [following the initial stage of awakening her *attention*] in this process: (1) The awakening of a *desire* for something better, vs. 7–15. (2) The awakening of a *conviction* of personal need, vs. 16–20. (3) The call for a *decision* to acknowledge Jesus as the Messiah, vs. 21–26. (4) The stimulus to *action* appropriate to the decision, vs. 28–30, 39–42." *Seventh-day Adventist Bible Commentary*, Volume 5, pp. 937–938.

4. Ellen G. White, *The Desire of Ages*, p. 184.

5. John Dybdahl, "Cross-Cultural Adaptation: How to Contextualize the Gospel, *Ministry*, November 1992.

6. *The Desire of Ages*, p. 187.

7. *Ibid.*, pp. 187–188.

8. *Ibid.*

9. *Ibid.*

10. Ellen G. White, *Steps to Christ*, p. 78.

11. *The Ministry of Healing*, p. 143 (italics supplied).

Chapter Eighteen
In the Spirit and Power of Elijah

"And Elijah came to all the people, and said, 'How long will you falter between two opinions? If the Lord is God, follow Him; but if Baal, follow him.' But the people answered him not a word."

—1 Kings 18:21

While we find it fairly easy to visualize how Christ's method of soul-winning could work with an attentive, appreciative audience of one, we tend to wonder, Is it universal and flexible enough to work with an entire culture—especially a decidedly *in*attentive and *un*appreciative one? If so, how would it need to be "contextualized" in order to fit such challenging circumstances?

Surely the prophet Elijah must have engaged in some version of this thought process as he considered the spiritual and moral decline of his own culture. While he didn't have the benefit of witnessing God's premier revelation of Himself and His "method" in Jesus Christ, he was intimately familiar with His character through his knowledge of the Scriptures and his own personal walk. So he must have wondered, as his heart was wrung by his people's headlong plunge into apostasy, How to get through to them in a way that was both consistent with the character of God and relevant to their circumstances? [1] How to bring them gospel healing when they adamantly maintained that they didn't even have a fatal disease? He would first need, as C.S. Lewis has said, "to preach the diagnosis—in itself very bad news" in order to "win a hearing for the cure."[2]

It was a difficult assignment that required a lot of careful discernment and sanctified finesse. Recognizing that a steady stream of "appeals, remonstrances, and warnings had failed to bring Israel to repentance,"[3] Elijah felt convicted to do something that on the surface seems very unchristlike. He prayed that God would "arrest the once-favored people in their wicked course, to visit them with judgments, if need be, that they might be led to see in its true light their departure from Heaven."[4] Yet if we think Elijah's strong medicine was harder on the patient than the disease itself, we underestimate the deadly virulence of unrestrained sin. In fact, God was the One who had inspired Elijah's expression of "tough love," and He honored it by withholding life-giving dew and rain in order to precipitate a needed state of crisis.[5]

When the crisis had fully developed at the end of three-and-a-half years of wasting drought and famine, Elijah challenged his weary people to meet with him on Mount Carmel, where he preached the "bad news" of their diagnosis of idolatry and double-mindedness. "How long will you falter between two opinions?" he bluntly confronted them; "If the Lord is God, follow Him; but if Baal, follow him" (1 Kings 18:21).

In what way were the people "faltering" between two opinions? On the one hand, they wanted the *enjoyment* of following Baal, whose sensual worship permitted them to retain their carnal natures; on the other hand, they wanted the *benefits* that come from being affiliated with God, who alone could provide for their needs and sustain their lives. They wanted to have their cake and eat it too, by being both religious *and* rebellious. Elijah, in confronting them with their deadly double-mindedness, was doing them a favor by *opening their eyes* to their underlying spiritual problem and placing squarely with them the responsibility for *choosing* what to do about it.

This is, in fact, the practical value of the doctrine of sin. As theologian Linda Mercadante has explained it, "The doctrine of sin seeks to preserve an element of *human responsibility and freedom*, even in the face of God's sovereignty and in light of radical evil."[6] Sin has both a binding and blinding effect, such that, as it sucks us into its undertow, we tend to forget that we still have a choice in the matter. "Preaching the diagnosis" reminds us that God has made us free moral agents who are responsible for our moral choices and their outcomes. It reminds us of the crucial, all-important role of the *will*, which must be awakened and engaged "if we are to return God's love for us in a voluntary, rather than a coerced or determined, manner."[7]

Not surprisingly, the Israelites' wills had become so compromised by sin, and they felt so intimidated by the corrupt leaders who had seduced them into ever deepening apostasy, that they "answered him not a word" (v. 21). Yet Elijah didn't castigate them for their timidity and unbelief. Recognizing that "the best reason to preach on sin is to highlight the power and joy of grace,"[8] he proceeded to lead his people to their gospel cure.

He began by arranging circumstances in a way that would enable them to make an informed choice, based on a distinct contrast. So he invited the priests of Baal, "Give us two bulls; and … choose one bull for [yourselves], cut it in pieces, and lay it on the wood, but put no fire under it; and I will prepare the other bull, and lay it on the wood, but put no fire under it. Then you call on the name of your gods, and I will call on the name of the Lord; and the God who answers by fire, He is God" (1 Kings 18:23, 24). His request was so reasonable and intriguing that the people were compelled to respond, "It is well spoken" (v. 24).

At this point, the social dynamics of the situation were such that the false prophets couldn't refuse his gauntlet without totally discrediting themselves. Grudgingly complying with his conditions, they cranked up their worship machine for a no-holds-barred performance. "Hear us, O Baal!" they wailed, as they "leaped about the altar which they had made" and "cut themselves, as was their custom, with knives and lances, until the blood gushed out on them" (vs. 26, 28). All day long, as the blistering sun sailed from one end of the white-hot horizon to the other, they raged and writhed like lunatics, in the process revealing the true character of their irrational, punitive god. [9] Finally, infuriated with their impassive deity, they "mingle[d] with their pleadings terrible cursings;"[10] yet, notwithstanding all of their frantic theatrics, "there was no voice; no one answered, no one paid attention" (v. 29).

Utterly defeated, the bleeding, mutilated priests fell panting to the ground at the time of the evening sacrifice. In the deafening calm that followed, Elijah quietly invited the people, "Come near to me" (v. 30). Expectantly they drew near, thoroughly disgusted and disillusioned by their priests' sensational but impotent intercessions. By contrast, the calm and compassionate demeanor of Elijah appealed to both their hearts and minds, and won their confidence. As they attentively watched, he reverently repaired God's broken altar, dug a trench about it, and positioned the sacrifice; then, amazingly, he invited the people to saturate the whole thing with water until the trench overflowed. Thus placing himself at a distinct disadvantage, he offered a simple but compelling prayer to the God he knew so well:

> "Lord God of Abraham, Isaac, and Israel, let it be known this day that *You* are God in Israel and I am Your servant, and that I have done all these things at Your word. Hear me, O Lord, hear me, that this people may *know* that You are the Lord God, and that You have *turned their hearts back to You again*" (vs. 36, 37, italics added).

In instant recognition of Elijah's simple prayer of faith, "the fire of the Lord fell and consumed the burnt sacrifice, and the wood and the stones and the dust, and it licked up the water that was in the trench" (v. 38). Awe-stricken, the people fell on their faces and, to a person, confessed, "The Lord, He is God! The Lord, He is God!" (v. 39, italics added). [11]

It is worth pausing here to note an important point that is lost in our English translation. The Hebrew word that the Israelites used for "Lord" is *Yehovah*, the "Self-existent or Eternal One," and is derived from the Hebrew *hayah*, the name that God used to describe Himself to Moses in Exodus 3:14: "I AM that I AM" (*hayah hayah*). [12] The people's use of this appellation indicates that they clearly distinguished now between their inferior, humanly contrived "god" Baal, and *Yehovah*, the superior, self-existent Creator of all things.

This is precisely the place to which Elijah had been trying to bring them, because it is the vantage point for repentance. Only as they stood in the awe-inspiring presence of the God who had made and sustained them could the Israelites intelligently sorrow for sin. Only then could they understand that sin, at its heart, is a self-centered, unreasoning rebellion against the holy, benevolent *Person* from whom our very existence derives. On such deep and thorough repentance is reconciliation based, and as they experienced it, their hearts were truly "turned back" to the only God who truly loved them.

So Elijah compellingly preached his prodigal people's diagnosis and won a hearing for the cure. It's a divinely inspired model of spiritual intervention that is, essentially, the method modeled by Christ—appropriately contextualized for a rebellious, inattentive culture.

God has promised that, just "before the coming of the great and dreadful day of the Lord," He will figuratively "reincarnate" Elijah in His end-time church—meaning that the "spirit and power" that distinguished his compassionately confrontational ministry will also distinguish theirs (Malachi 4:5; Luke 1:17). [13] In practical terms, this means that, like Elijah:

- They will care enough about the alarming condition of their world to love it with "tough love," prayerfully interceding that, whatever it takes, God would intervene to bring it to its spiritual senses.

- They will provide people with a clear choice by not only articulating, but also powerfully *demonstrating*, God's character of *agape* in distinct contrast to the character of Satan, which permeates all of his spiritual and humanistic counterfeits.

- They will emphasize God's role as *Creator* and *Sustainer*, that people who have lost sight of this truth may *remember* who made them, who loves them, and to whom they're accountable.

- They will both compellingly convict of sin and complimentarily "highlight the power and joy" of its gospel solution.

All of this they will do in order to "turn the hearts of the fathers to the children, and the hearts of the children to their fathers"—to be, in their dying, alienated world, the reviving "spirit and power" of *reconciliation*, that a people may be prepared to meet their soon-coming God (Malachi 4:6; see Amos 4:12).

Endnotes

1. To get the full story, read 1 Kings 16:29–18:46.

2. C.S. Lewis, *The Problem of Pain* (HarperCollins Publishers, Inc., 1996), p. 48.

3. Ellen. G. White, *Prophets and Kings*, p. 120.

4. *Ibid.*

5. Elijah's prayer and God's response were consistent with the Lord's earlier injunction to the Israelites through Moses, "Take heed to yourselves, lest your heart be deceived, and you turn aside and serve other gods and worship them, lest the Lord's anger be aroused against you, and *He shut up the heavens so that there be no rain*, and the land

yield no produce, and you perish quickly from the good land which the Lord is giving you" (Deuteronomy 11:16, 17, italics added). Actually, this forcing of a crisis is not unknown even to secular minds. It's a well-known technique in drug rehabilitation circles, where it is appropriately called an "intervention." While excruciatingly difficult for all involved, it is performed for the good of the addicted person and their family.

6. Linda A. Mercadante, "Sin, Addiction, and Freedom," in *Reconstructing Christian Theology*, eds. Rebecca S. Chopp and Mark Lewis Taylor (Minneapolis: Fortress Press, 1994), p. 230 (italics supplied). Please see this chapter for a very helpful discussion on the meaning of sin, its "medicalization," and the need for developing a morally, psychologically, physiologically, and sociologically integrated approach to addressing it.

7. *Ibid.*, p. 232.

8. "Sin, Addiction, and Freedom," p. 240.

9. Who was, in essence, Satan.

10. *Prophets and Kings*, p. 150.

11. Note that it was the "people" who repented and responded positively. Their corrupt leaders, hardened in rebellion, became God's implacable enemies. Such is the polarizing effect of undiluted truth.

12. From Strong's Exhaustive Concordance: "1961. hayah, haw-yaw'; a prim. root … to exist, i.e. be or become, come to pass (always emphatic, and not a mere copula or auxiliary);" and "3068. Yehovah, yeh-ho-vaw'; from H1961; (the) self-Existent or Eternal; Jeho-vah, Jewish national name of God:—Jehovah, the Lord."

13. This also describes the ministry of John the Baptist, the First Advent embodiment of "the spirit and power of Elijah," who confronted his people with their need to repent of their sins, and directed their attention to the "the Lamb of God who *takes away* the sin of the world" (Luke 1:17; John 1:29, italics added).

Revival's Grand Conclusion

Chapter Nineteen
A Most Precious Message

"The Lord in his great mercy sent a most precious message to his people through Elders Waggoner and Jones. This message was to bring more prominently before the world the uplifted Saviour, the sacrifice for the sins of the whole world. It presented justification through faith in the Surety; it invited the people to receive the righteousness of Christ, which is made manifest in obedience to all the commandments of God."

—Ellen G. White,
Testimonies to Ministers and Gospel Workers[1]

In their book *Relativism*, Francis J. Beckwith and Gregory Koukl bemoan the "profound moral illiteracy"[2] of contemporary culture. It's a tragedy the latter eloquently captures as he relates a conversation he had with a medical assistant who prepped him for an exam. Their dialogue was as follows:

" 'Can I ask you a personal question?' I asked. She paused in her work, uncertain how to respond. 'I'm reading a book on ethics, and I want to know your opinion about something.'

" 'Oh,' she said. 'Okay.'

" 'Do you believe that morality is absolute, or do all people decide for themselves?'

" 'What do you mean by morality?' she asked.

" 'Simply put, what's right and what's wrong,' I answered.

"We talked back and forth for a few minutes, and it became evident to me that she was having a difficult time even comprehending the questions I was asking about moral categories. I thought maybe a clear-case example would make the task simpler, a question with an obvious answer, such as, Who is buried in Grant's tomb? or, How long was the Hundred Years War?

" 'Is murder wrong?' I asked. 'Is it wrong to take an innocent human life?'

"She waffled. 'Well …'

" 'Well … what?'

" 'Well, I'm thinking.'

"I was surprised at her hesitation. 'What I'm trying to find out is whether morals, right and wrong, are something we make up for ourselves or something we discover. In other words, do morals apply whether we believe in them or not?'

"I waited. 'Can we say that taking innocent life is morally acceptable?'

" 'I guess it depends,' she said tentatively.

" 'Depends on what?' I asked.

" 'It depends on what other people think or decide.'

"'I'll make this really easy, I thought. 'Do you think torturing babies for fun is wrong?'

" 'Well … I wouldn't want them to do that to my baby.'

" 'You've missed the point of my question,' I said, a bit exasperated. 'I may not like burned food, but that doesn't mean giving it to me is immoral. Do you believe there is any circumstance, in any culture, at any time in history, in which torturing babies just for pure pleasure could be justified? Is it objectively wrong, or is it just a matter of opinion?'

"There was a long pause. Finally she answered, 'People should all be allowed to decide for themselves.'"[3]

While this disturbing anecdote is representative of an extremely relativistic, even morally apathetic mind-set,[4] it emphasizes a fact about which we've all become painfully aware: We live in an increasingly morally insensate and anarchical culture that, not only tends *not* to "do the right thing," but doesn't even seem to understand what the "right thing" *is*. It's a truly deplorable postmodern[5] tragedy that ought to give us a whopping case of righteous indignation. Yet even as we do right to righteously deplore it, our indignation tends to be accompanied by a bad case of nostalgia for what we romanticize as the "good old days" of law and order.

For Adventists, those good old, law-abiding days tend to be envisioned as the era of our early pioneers, when life, both inside and outside the church, operated like a predictable, well-oiled machine that was appropriately subject to the laws of physics and good behavior. Yet while we do well to appreciate the contributions and very real sacrifices of our forebears, we also need to candidly recognize that, as is the case with us, they had their spiritual and personal challenges. With the passage of years they succumbed to the all-too-human tendency to unconsciously drift into spiritual autopilot, formally going through the memorized motions of religion even while the inner flame of deep devotion was slowly becoming extinguished.

Such was the relatively sterile condition of our church by the 1880s, a period that, according to Adventist historian and theologian Herbert Douglass, "many [inspired] references describe ... in bleak terms":

> "Our church, generally, had drifted into a legalistic experience, holding fast to their commandment keeping. But a rich, Spirit-filled life—a heart religion—that moves people from one victory

over sin to another, from self-centeredness to a generous, loving person, was sadly lacking."[6]

Ellen White concurs in her now-famous 1890 lament, "As a people, we have preached the law until we are as dry as the hills of Gilboa that had neither dew nor rain,"[7] and she affirms that the world had good reason to perceive that "Seventh-day Adventists talk the law, the law, but do not teach or believe Christ."[8] Because the church had not yet embraced and conveyed a mature, comprehensive understanding of the gospel, "the *world* had not yet been given a fair picture of what the messages of the three angels (Revelation 14) were meant to be. Therefore, the great need for a re-emphasis of the 'everlasting gospel' within the setting of 1888."[9]

This "re-emphasis"—not merely of the partially recovered Reformation gospel, but of the complete "everlasting gospel"— began to be articulated to the church in the late 1880s by God's "delegated messengers"[10] E.J. Waggoner and A.T. Jones. It is eloquently summarized by Ellen White in these words:

> "The Lord in his great mercy sent a most precious message to His people through Elders Waggoner and Jones. This message was to bring more prominently before the world the uplifted Saviour, the sacrifice for the sins of the whole world. It presented justification through faith in the Surety; it invited the people to receive the righteousness of Christ, which is made manifest in obedience to all the commandments of God. Many had lost sight of Jesus. They needed to have their eyes directed to His divine person, His merits, and His changeless love for the human family. All power is given into His hands, that He may dispense rich gifts unto men, imparting the priceless gift of His own righteousness to the

helpless human agent. *This is the message that God commanded to be given to the world. It is the third angel's message, which is to be proclaimed with a loud voice, and attended with the outpouring of His Spirit in a large measure."* [11]

If we were never given any other explanation of the so-called "1888 Message" than this astonishingly comprehensive paragraph, we would be infinitely blessed! It's a practical and symmetrical summarization of the paradoxical relationship between law and grace, obedience and faith, Sacrifice and Surety, justification and sanctification. And it's a nutshell representation of the practical and symmetrical "most precious message" as presented in 1888 and the years immediately following by Jones and Waggoner, and of course, Ellen White herself. [12]

And what was it that made this message so powerfully practical and balanced? *Christ* was its center and substance; in *Him* truth's apparently contradictory poles adhered and blended into a seamless, integrated unity. As theologian A. Leroy Moore has encapsulated it, "Christ is *Himself* the law revealed as well as grace embodied. It is this *fusion*, which results only when the focus is upon Him for Whom the law is a transcript and grace its expression, which was the driving force behind the 1888 message." [13] Ellen White agrees as she later references her above paragraph: "This is the testimony that must go throughout the length and breadth of the world. It presents *the law and the gospel, binding up the two in a perfect whole."* [14]

As articulated in the 1888 message, Christ is the "Gestalt" of the gospel, the living whole who is greater than the sum of His theological "parts." He is the gravitational hub that holds in obedient orbit the paradoxical elements which, when left to our management, only repel and even destroy each other. In Him, law and gospel, faith and works, assurance and perfection, and every other apparent theological oxymoron settle their circular argument with a kiss of peace (which means that as we truly abide in Him, all of *our* circular theological arguments will do the same).

As our spiritual eyes are directed to "His divine person, His merits, and His changeless love for the human family"— "if we do not interpose a perverse will and frustrate His grace"[15] —He *will* give us the rich gift of His cleansing, empowering righteousness, which alone can bring us into a state of appreciative submission. The love of Christ, received into the soul, will enable us to magnify and obediently fulfill the law in the most real and practical sense. *This* is "the third angel's message in verity"[16] —the "message God commanded to be given to the *world*." It's the only one that is comprehensive and compelling enough to spark and sustain the kind of revival that will ripen the soul harvest of the earth.

We are right to conclude that our relativistic world needs law. But it needs "*Christ* in the law"—*then* "there will be sap and nourishment in the preaching that will be as food to the famishing flock."[17] A return to the "good old days" of Christless law and order would be putting a band-aid on a mortal wound. We can't go back. Like a woman in travail, the church must push into the pain of living in this morally chaotic world, and, by the grace of God, deliver from its ruins a new and vital experience that will carry all who share in it straight into the arms of our gloriously returning Savior.

Endnotes

1. Ellen G. White, *Testimonies to Ministers and Gospel Workers*, pp. 91–92.

2. Francis J. Beckwith and Gregory Koukl, *Relativism: Feet Firmly Planted in Mid-Air* (Grand Rapids, MI: Baker Books, 1998), p. 34.

3. *Ibid.*, pp. 34–35.

4. Although the woman's sense of right and wrong intuitively kicked in when she personalized this gruesome scenario by placing her own baby at the center of it.

5. While postmodernism is regarded as a late 20th century philosophical, ethical, and social phenomenon in its own right, it is the natural progeny of its predecessor

modernism (or modernity), which, while it adhered to some semblance of morality, held that this morality derived from the rational assumptions and perceptions of the subjective self, not from an immutable God. It would seem that postmodernism is the inevitable discovery that the fallen, subjective self can never originate or independently perceive absolute, objective truth.

6. Herbert E. Douglass, *Should We Ever Say, "I Am Saved"?* (Nampa, ID: Pacific Press Publishing Association, 2003), p. 96.

7. Ellen G. White, *Testimonies to the Church*, Volume 6, p. 417.

8. *Testimonies to Minsters and Gospel Workers*, p. 92; note that this was written eight years after the introduction to the church of the "1888 Message," indicating that, for the most part, the complete teaching of Christ our Righteousness had not been embraced.

9. *Should We Ever Say, "I Am Saved"?*, p. 96 (italics supplied).

10. *Testimonies to Minsters and Gospel Workers*, p. 97.

11. *Ibid.*, pp. 91–92 (italics added). The essence of the message can be gleaned from the following materials: *Steps to Christ, Christ's Object Lessons, The Desire of Ages, Thoughts From the Mount of Blessing, Faith and Works, Testimonies to Minsters and Gospel Workers* (pp. 63–81, 89–98, 464–469), and *The Ellen G. White 1888 Materials* by Ellen G. White; *The Consecrated Way* by A.T. Jones and his sermons in the *1895 General Conference Bulletin* (though both of these may contain some tendencies toward perfectionism, which is an imbalanced approach toward Christian perfection); *Christ and His Righteousness* and *Waggoner on Romans* by E. J. Waggoner; *In Search of the Cross* by Robert J. Wieland; *A Most Precious Message* by Jennifer Jill Schwirzer. See also *Christ Our Righteousness* by A.G. Daniels, and *Adventism in Conflict* by A. Leroy Moore (pp. 77–126) for a discussion of the theological issues.

12. It's important to note that Jones and Waggoner, while used of God, were flawed human instruments (as are we all) who required occasional course corrections that the Lord supplied through Ellen White. It is to their credit that, in the early years of their ministry, they generally responded positively to her reproofs. It's tragic that, in their later years, they drifted into questionable paths, though this does not discredit the biblical emphases they shared while still walking in the light.

13. A Leroy Moore, from a personal email exchange dated August 13, 2004 (italics added).

14. *Testimonies to Minsters and Gospel Workers*, p. 94 (italics added).

15. Ellen G. White, *Thoughts From the Mount of Blessing*, p. 76.

16. Ellen G. White, *Review and Herald*, April 1, 1890.

17. *Testimonies to the Church*, Volume 6, p. 417 (italics added).

Chapter Twenty
God's Final Generation

"Christ is waiting with longing desire for the manifestation of Himself in His church. When the character of Christ shall be perfectly reproduced in His people, then He will come to claim them as His own."
—Ellen G. White, *Christ's Object Lessons* [1]

J ohn Wesley, the great eighteenth century revivalist and reformer, once said something very sobering about revival. He said:

> "I do not see how it is possible, in the nature of things, for any revival of religion to continue long. For religion must necessarily produce both industry and frugality, and these cannot but produce riches. But as riches increase, so will pride, anger, and love of the world in all its branches." [2]

Such has been the pattern of revival throughout history: As we come to the end of our ropes and in desperation reach out to God, He graciously saves us and turns us into disciplined, virtuous people who, in turn, create a world in which we become so comfortable and successful that we conclude we must not have needed Him very much after all! In other words, Christianity, as it's generally practiced, tends to work itself out of a job—on both an individual and collective level. Yet does this mean that we (and God) must "pragmatically" give up hoping it could be otherwise, and simply ride the revival roller coaster until His cosmic clock strikes 12:00 and He roars back—ready or not—to wreak vengeance on our rogue planet?

While this scenario appeals to our natural sense of irresponsibility, we've been assured by inspiration that there will come a time when it will be otherwise—when the "most precious message" of revival will take such deep and tenacious root in the hearts of those who receive it, that it will continue to bud and burst forth until it finds its final fruitage in an abundant end time harvest of souls:

> The work will be similar to that of the Day of Pentecost. As the "former rain" was given, in the outpouring of the Holy Spirit at the opening of the gospel, to cause the upspringing of the precious seed, so the "latter rain" will be given at its close for the ripening of the harvest. ... The rays of light penetrate everywhere, the truth is seen in its clearness, and the honest children of God sever the bands which have held them. ... Notwithstanding the agencies combined against the truth, a *large number* take their stand upon the Lord's side. [3]

What a wonderful assurance! God has promised that there will come a time when revival will so thoroughly do its work of transformation and reformation that it will not die on the vine, but will culminate in the calling out of a people prepared for the second coming of Christ. The "honest children of God" will, once and for all, "get it," such that they will never again be enamored of "riches ... pride, anger, and love of the world" in any of its seductive forms. They will no longer experience revival as a mere means to a self-interested end, but will recognize in it an ongoing opportunity to glorify God and bless their fellow beings. Such will be the mature experience of the "final generation" of believers gathered out of the world.

And this brings us to a question that's inevitably asked when the subject of the "final generation" comes up: Is it some kind of exclusive fraternity of elite Christians, who are somehow made of holier or sterner stuff than we? It's a question that, in turn, inevitably lead us into a head-on collision with that old Adventist bugaboo—*perfection*. It's a word we can't avoid, considering the topic. So let's start our discussion with a classic quote that always manages to stir the perfection pot:

> "Christ is waiting with longing desire for the manifestation of Himself in His church. When the character of Christ shall be *perfectly reproduced* in His people, then He will come to claim them as His own." [4]

This statement has fueled endless perfection debates, delighting the idealistically confident few and discouraging the (perhaps more realistic) many, who, as they survey their uneven Christian experience and deceitful hearts, despair of ever reaching such a lofty goal. While better books than this one have dealt more clearly and comprehensively with this controversial topic, [5] we wouldn't be doing the subject of this chapter justice if we didn't address it. So let's start by summarizing what Christian perfection is *not*.

It's *not* something that makes people mean and exclusive and denunciatory toward those who don't "measure up" to its exalted standards. It's not a strained and stoic imitation of Christ, who, it envisions, became "just like" us that we may become, (and have no excuse *not* to become), "just like" Him. It doesn't constitute the currency of our salvation or the substance of our assurance. In short, it's not the heresy of perfection*ism*, which is a neurotic, self-defeating obsession with performance that turns its devotees into "twofold more the child of hell" than they were before they succumbed to the dreadful malady.[6]

As good as such perfectionism might sound, and even *look* on a good day, it's the theological and practical equivalent of a beautiful butterfly preserved in amber—apparently exquisite in every detail, but also very dead. Rather, the inspired doctrine of Christian perfection is just that—*inspired*, dynamic, full of life, and generously mindful of the fragility of its human vessel. This is not at all to say that it excuses sin, but that it realistically recognizes the nature of the clay into which it's been worked. It never asks for more than we can practically experience, at any given time in our Christian development, in Christ.

And this is the key to Christian perfection—*in Christ*. The starting point for revival is also its finish, as Christ our Righteousness is both the "author and *finisher* of our faith" (Hebrews 12:2). The journey of faith that we *began* in Him, we continually *live* in Him, and will ultimately *conclude* in Him. It is *His* grace that brought us salvation, *His* goodness that leads us into an ever-deepening repentance, *His* Spirit that continually transforms us into His image, *His* Word that sustains us. Christ is the very contents of, and the divine parentheses around, our Christian experience. Christian perfection is nothing more or less than abiding in Christ, continually growing up into the image of the One in whose perfect image we were born again. This is why it can be said:

> At every stage of development our life may be *perfect*; yet if God's purpose for us is fulfilled, there will be continual advancement. ... By constantly relying upon Christ as our personal Saviour, we shall grow up into Him in all things who is our head.[7]

Such an understanding of perfection will never undermine our assurance of salvation and security in Christ. It should rather encourage us to recognize that Christ makes it *His* business to bring to maturation the life He implanted within us, and that our relatively minor, though crucial, role is to appreciatively *cooperate* with Him. Such is the perfection that has been experienced by God's committed people throughout history, and such it will be for God's final generation.

Having said that, we must also recognize that this group of believers will experience Christian perfection in a unique, extremely rigorous apocalyptic *context* that has been frequently foreshadowed throughout history, but has never actually *happened* before. While "that which has been," in terms of the great controversy between good and evil, "will be" yet again, "the coming struggle will be marked with a terrible *intensity* such as the world has never witnessed."[8] Never before have the powers of light and darkness climactically clashed and wrestled for the mastery through every living soul. Never before has an entire, technologically sophisticated, psychologically savvy *planet* singled out and implacably vilified one comparatively small group of scapegoats whom it charges with its utter ruin. Never before has the moderating, sin-restraining influence of the Holy Spirit been withdrawn from a whole world full of people who have decidedly and irreversibly rejected it.[9]

And what will make this end-time intensity even more challenging for this conscientious, besieged body of believers to bear is the disturbing sense "that they have brought [about] the crisis"[10] by simply sharing with others the good news that has so warmed their own hearts. Altogether, it's a white-hot apocalyptic crucible that will compel those who experience it to be utterly honest with themselves about their motives, and absolutely intentional about their choice to identify with Christ in a perplexing world that professes to love Him, but at heart hates everything that He's about. It's an ordeal that will continually confront God's people with their native inability to cope, and so drive them ever more snugly into the arms of the only One who can strengthen them to bear it—not for the sake of their own salvation, which is not in question, but for His honor, and for the sake of their fellow believers.

This brings us to the most defining characteristic of the "perfection" of God's final generation: Far from being the stuff of individualist obsession, it is the substance of *collectivist* concern. While perfection*ism* focuses our eyes on self and so increases our insecurity and self-centeredness, true Christian perfection *loses* itself in loving others, in humbly incarnating Christ to them. As Leroy Moore has observed, "Perfection cannot occur in isolation. Independence accentuates human selfishness and breeds egocentricity. To counteract that egocentricity, we must humble ourselves one to another within the body." [11]

How could we expect it to be otherwise? God, who is perfect love, does not experience that perfection as a solitary entity but as a three-fold family, whose members continually engage in a joyful reciprocity of sublime self-giving. Patterned after Him, we are "made perfect in love" (1 John 4:18), not in self-sufficient isolation but in self-forgetful interaction, because while "grace is always a present possibility for individuals … its flow comes to fullness through community." [12]

So the corporate awareness of this last generation will stretch to take in the *entire* community of Christ, which comprehends *all* who have ever joined it. [13] Yearning to see released from their graves those who have gone before, who "died in faith, not having received the promises, but having seen them afar off," recognizing that God has planned it so that "they should not be made perfect apart from us," they determine to cooperate with Him in bringing closure to the Great Controversy (Hebrews 11:13, 12:1). Far from perceiving themselves as an elite group of gifted virtuosos who exceed the performance of their predecessors, they envision themselves as the anchormen and women of a committed team of relay runners, who want only, by the grace of God, to faithfully carry to the finish line the baton that has been placed in their feeble hands. Such corporate perfection is truly a perfection for the ages in that it is a *maturation*, or *completion*, not only of the characters of those who personally experience it, but of the *church*. It's the decisive culmination of 6,000 long years of erratic revival and reformation ebb and flow. It's the "perfect" conclusion for which Christ waits with longing desire, that He may return and be forever united with every person who has ever loved Him throughout history—who *altogether* constitute His beloved bride, the church.

Endnotes

1. Ellen G. White, *Christ's Object Lessons*, p. 69.

2. As quoted by Philip Yancey in "Forgetting God: Why Decadence Drives Out Discipline," *Christianity Today* online; at http://www.christianitytoday.com/ct/2004/009/21.104.html

3. Ellen G. White, *The Great Controversy*, pp. 611–612 (italics added).

4. *Christ's Object Lessons*, p. 69 (italics added).

5. For a helpful discussion of the difference between Christian perfection and perfectionism, see J.R. Zurcher, *Christian Perfection*; A. Leroy Moore, *Adventism in Conflict* (pp. 158–180); Marvin Moore, *How to Think About the End Time* (pp. 170–190); and Herbert E. Douglass, *Should We Ever Say, "I Am Saved"?* (pp. 104–115).

6. I know this because, when it comes to perfectionism, I'm the chief of offenders.

7. *Christ's Object Lessons*, pp. 65, 67 (italics added).

8. *The Great Controversy*, p. 11 (italics added).

9. It is a misnomer, however, to conclude that God's Spirit will be withdrawn from His people, who would never for a moment be able to maintain their Christian experience without its indwelling presence. "The idea that after the close of probation God will remove His Spirit from His people, leaving them to battle Satan alone, is *simply not true*. It is the wicked who will suffer the loss of His presence. A statement by Ellen White ... is worth repeating here: 'When He [Christ] leaves the sanctuary, darkness covers the inhabitants of the earth. In that fearful time the righteous must live in the sight of a holy God without an intercessor. *The restraint which has been upon the wicked is removed*, and Satan has entire control of the finally impenitent ... *The Spirit of God, persistently resisted, has been at last withdrawn*.'" Marvin Moore, *How To Think About the End Time* (Nampa, ID: Pacific Press Publishing Association, 2001), p. 187, italics included in original.

10. *The Great Controversy*, p. 610.

11. A. Leroy Moore, *Adventism in Conflict* (Hagerstown, MD: Review and Herald Publishing Association, 1995), p. 160.

12. Gerald G. May, M.D., *Addiction and Grace* (New York: HarperCollins Publishers, 1988), p. 52.

13. Which, of course, includes all of those who, throughout history, have "intuitively" worshiped Christ, without benefit of literal exposure to biblical teachings. (See Romans 2:13–15; Zechariah 13:6.)

Chapter Twenty-One
Revival's Glorious Climax

> *"The cross of Christ will be the science and the song of the redeemed throughout eternity. In Christ glorified they will behold Christ crucified. Never will it be forgotten that He whose power created and upheld the unnumbered worlds ... humbled Himself to uplift fallen man; that He bore the guilt and shame of sin, and the hiding of His Father's face, till the woes of a lost world broke His heart and crushed out His life on Calvary's cross."*
> —Ellen G. White, *The Great Controversy*[1]

It's the climactic moment the universe has waited 6,000 years to witness. The moment when the meek and lowly "Lamb slain from the foundation of the world" returns as a kingly, conquering Lion to "ransom" His sleeping saints "from the power of the grave," and rescue from their tormentors His waiting ones (Revelation 13:8; Hosea 13:14). As "dense blackness, deeper than the darkness of the night"[2] envelopes the reeling, convulsing earth, a small patch of sky explodes into transcendent, consuming light. At its center, surrounded by "ten thousand times ten thousand" ecstatically singing angels, Jesus sits gloriously enthroned, poised to translate His besieged kingdom of grace into an eternally triumphant kingdom of glory (Daniel 7:10).

First the sleeping ones are released from their prison house of death, "in a moment, in the twinkling of an eye," at the life-giving sound of their Savior's familiar voice (1 Corinthians 15:52). Then the bodies and minds of the waiting ones thrill with immortal vigor as they are transformed into His glorified likeness. Having transcended the limitations of time and death, fully and finally united, the members of the body of Christ are rapturously "caught up together ... in the clouds to meet the Lord in the air: and so shall [they] ever be with the Lord" (1 Thessalonians 4:17 KJV).

It's the joyous dawning of the eternal day for which "the whole creation" even now "groans and labors with birth pangs" (Romans 8:22)! Never again will God's people be subject to the ravages of death and disease; never again will they be tormented by the evil one. Carried on the wings of angels to the heavenly City of God, their glorified senses are ravished by the resplendent beauty of it all—by the breathtaking sight of Eden restored, by the entrancing sound of music that seems to emanate from the very air, by the pungent scent of thriving, luxuriant life!

More than this, they are unspeakably delighted to see "those who have been won to Christ through their prayers, their labors, and their loving sacrifice."[3] It's a delight that is multiplied many times over as they "see that one has gained others, and these still others, all brought into the haven of rest."[4]—a reward greater even than all the beauties of heaven combined.

And at the center of it all is Jesus, like a radiant diamond set in the heart of a delicate diadem—the One who has made it all possible, without whom heaven would not be heaven. As the jubilant multitude are magnetically drawn to His shining form, every eye gazes lovingly at His benevolent face, and every voice spontaneously breaks forth into appreciative praise: "To *Him* who loved us and washed us from our sins in His own blood, and has made us kings and priests to His God and Father, to *Him* be glory and dominion forever and ever!" (Revelation 1:5–6, italics supplied). It's a heartfelt refrain that will rapturously echo through the graceful hills and valleys throughout the endless ages, as the redeemed ever remember at whose expense they enjoy this eternity of bliss:

> The cross of Christ will be the science and the song of the redeemed throughout eternity. In Christ glorified they will behold Christ crucified. Never will it be forgotten that He whose power created and upheld the unnumbered worlds through the vast realms of space, the Beloved of God, the Majesty of heaven, He whom cherub and seraph delighted to adore—humbled Himself to uplift fallen man; that He bore the guilt and shame of sin, and the hiding of His Father's face, till the woes of a lost world broke His heart and crushed out His life on Calvary's cross.[5]

Though we've been there ten thousand times ten thousand years, we will "ever have a distinct, intelligent knowledge of what [our] salvation has cost."[6] The passage of endless ages will never dim, but only intensify our appreciative awareness that, because "He suffered the death which was ours," we "receive the life which was His"[7]—that we may be *eternally* revived, and ever and always *live* in His sight.

Endnotes

1. Ellen G. White, *The Great Controversy*, p. 651

2. *Ibid.*, p. 636.

3. *Ibid.*, p. 647.

4. *Ibid.*

5. *Ibid.*, p. 651.

6. *Ibid.*

7. Ellen G. White, *The Desire of Ages*, p. 25.

Don't miss our FREE online
Bible Prophecy course at
www.bibleuniverse.com
Enroll today and
expand your universe!